Sinéad O'Connor
So Different

Dermott Hayes

OMNIBUS PRESS
LONDON · NEW YORK · SYDNEY

Edited by Chris Charlesworth
Cover designed by Lisa Pettibone/Four Corners Design
Cover photograph by Steve Double
Book designed by Four Corners Design
Picture research by Dermott Hayes & Dave Brolan
Project co-ordination by Caroline Watson

ISBN 0.7119.2482.1
Order No. OP 46226

Exclusive distributors:
Book Sales Limited,
8/9 Frith Street,
London W1V 5TZ.

Music Sales Corporation,
225 Park Avenue South,
New York, NY 10003, USA.

Music Sales Pty Ltd.,
120 Rothschild Avenue,
Rosebery, NSW 2018, Australia.

To the Music Trade only:
Music Sales Limited,
8/9 Frith Street,
London W1V 5TZ, UK.

Typeset on Quark Express 3.0 by Four Corners Design

Printed by BPCC Hazell Books, Aylesbury, Bucks

Picture credits:
Fergus Bourke: 10; Cyril Byrne: 52, 56, 101; Charles
Collins: 66, 90 ; Joey Cleary: 63; George Chin: 98;
Steve Double: front cover, 4, 6, 9, 12, 30, 35, 54,
71t&b, 73t&b, 85; Colman Doyle: 76; Robert Doyle:
126b; Columb Farrelly: 11t; Colm Henry: 21, 22, 24,
42, 43t, 55, 91, 96t&b, 97, 102; Des Harris: 28; Irish
Press Newspapers: 53t, 69, 74, 81, 103; London
Features International: 18, 51, 58, 61, 64; Zak Martin:
13, 17, 19, 31, 32, 43b; Mike Morton: 104t&b, 105;
Aiden O'Keef: 124, 125, 126t; Pictorial Press: 53b, 83,
89, 94, 114, 120, 121t; Redferns: 48, 82, 88t&b, 99,
108, 109, 110t; Relay: 107b, 121b, 123; Retna: 50, 65,
84, 93, 107t; Derek Spiers: 79, 80, 115; Starfile: 67;
Toni Thomson: 16.

Contents

Introduction

Sigmund Freud believed there is no truth to be found in biography. I'm not here to trade psychoses with him. Truth, like beauty, is in the eye of the beholder.

This is an unofficial biography of Sinéad O'Connor, rock singer, composer and musician. An enigmatic Irish genius, she is riddled and blessed by the contradictions of her appearance and style, her life and the life of her own people, the Irish.

It suffers and benefits from the lack of official co-operation. The author has met Sinéad O'Connor on four occasions. The first was at a Pogues' concert at the Brixton Academy, London, on St. Patrick's night, 1987. The second was in a Dublin hotel, the day after her secret marriage to John Reynolds, the father of her son, Jake. The third was on New Year's Eve, 1989, in Dublin's Point Theatre, when U2 brought their 'Lovetown' tour to their hometown.

The last occasion was a sometimes vicious and revealing stand-up row in a Dublin bar on November 12, 1990.

To tell the whole truth, some people argue, you must have all the facts. But who can ever say they have all the facts? *So Different* is a modest attempt to illuminate some of the less well clarified facts about Sinéad's background, to find the source of the myths that have grown up around her, either by her own efforts or through the imagination of those who have written about her.

The purpose is to shed some light on the well spring of her talent, her work and her genius. It is not to titillate or destroy or cast aspersions and shadows over one of the brightest, incandescent stars of today.

A fire burns inside Sinéad O'Connor that is fuelled by her emotions, her experiences and her art. *So Different* is a search for the spark that lit the flame. It is a 'work-in-progress' in the sense that the Sinéad O'Connor story is only beginning. It is important that its illustration should begin now before it gets lost in the myths of time.

There are a few people who should be mentioned for without them none of this would have been possible ... To my loving and tolerant lover and wife, Toni and our beautiful daughters, Hannah and Holly.

Special thanks to my editor, Chris Charlesworth; to George Murray for letting me wade through his back issues of *Hot Press* in his Wicklow St. record shop; to all the people interviewed: Kieran Owens, Joe Falvey, Kevin O'Byrne, Columb Farrelly, Jeannette Byrne, Paul Byrne and assorted others who, for one reason or another, wished to remain anonymous.

More thanks to the tireless workers of the World Rock News Network, particularly Jonathan Ashby in London and Dave Alpert in New York.

The Myths Of Time

Slip the cassette into the VCR, sit back and rewind. Flashing images of that shaven head, the black tutu, the Doc Marten's … the dancing figure, alone on-stage with a tape machine … the face contorted in a muted anguished scream … a close-up of a sublime beauty in full-frontal victim pose and a solitary tear … STOP. REWIND.

That's it. The tear, that tear. The tear that launched six million albums. Sinéad O'Connor is singing 'Nothing Compares 2U' and you're transfixed, appalled, devastated. Because she's crying in a video and her soaring voice is just a decibel away from a sobbing wail. You want to hold her and comfort her and tell her it will be all right and no-one will ever make her cry again.

Then you stop and look again. REWIND. Look for the strings attached, the plate of chopped onions, whatever they use. This is artifice, this is pop music, showbusiness, performance art. People don't cry for real … or do they?

Sinéad O'Connor has always created her own myths. As a schoolgirl she was Cathy in *Wuthering Heights*, St. Bernadette at Lourdes, Joan of Arc at the burning stake, the ultimate victim.

She is a study in contradictions – Madonna and whore; innocent and knowing; a mother and child. As a teenager she pursued stardom with a vengeance, only to declare it an empty ideal when it lay spread out in front of her.

She is an intensely private person who bares her soul and intimate secrets in her music. She is an enigma whose life is an open book.

She has no message for the world but she wants to get on-stage to teach us.

Bob Dylan has spent a lifetime weaving myths around himself, protecting himself from the slings and arrows and poison pens by rewriting his entire life and upbringing. Even his age is in doubt, he says.

Sinéad O'Connor's background is equally mythical. Not because what we know is untrue but because her dramatic life story has been repeated so often and in such detail, it is no longer clear where truth ends and fiction takes over, where the mundane becomes fantastic.

Celebrity magnifies life. Rock stars and their publicists are well aware of the value of myth and mystery. In one sense an exciting and intriguing life can add to the aura of their fame and attraction. A life shrouded in mystery leaves everything to the imagination. Fiction can protect reality.

Fame, notoriety and stardom shine a light of scrutiny where none may ever have been lit. Had, for example, the young Robert Zimmerman settled down to run his family business in Hibbing, Minnesota, or had Sinéad O'Connor, God forbid, become a housewife, then no intrusive light would have shone down on either.

Chapter One

Success has made Sinéad O'Connor famous and fame has made her life an open book.

Her career so far has been marked by incredible bursts of creativity and soul baring, followed by bouts of publicity and controversy that are a testament to a compulsive desire to be in the limelight (though she says she hates it) and to explain herself in interviews (though she claims she is frequently misquoted and manipulated).

Sinéad believes interviews have nothing to do with selling records and everything to do with selling newspapers, yet in three years she has generated enough news copy to paper the White House.

Her story is relatively well known – born in Dublin of middle class parents who split up when she was eight. The trauma of the split caused her problems. She had trouble in school, played truant and became involved in petty theft.

She ran away from her mother and went to live with her father. She was in a succession of schools including a school for girls with behavioural problems when she was 14.

That year she sang at the wedding of one of her teachers and was approached by the brother of the bride who had just started a band and was struck by the power and quality of her voice. He invited her to join them in some recording sessions and later to help them with the writing of a song. The song, 'Take My Hand', was later recorded by the band In Tua Nua and used by them on their first EP for Island Records.

Sinéad was then sent to a boarding school in Waterford where she began to develop her singing and writing skills. On a summer break she joined a band called Ton Ton Macoute and, while still attending the boarding school, found time to gig and rehearse with them at weekends. She was spotted singing and playing with the band in a Dublin club by Ensign Records' bosses, Nigel Grainge and Chris Hill. They weren't interested in the band but they liked the singer.

Sinéad left the school in Waterford before her final exams to pursue her dream of a career in music. She contacted Grainge and headed for London. Ensign gave her a publishing deal and put her in a studio to begin work on her first album with veteran producer Mick Glossop.

Six months later this work was abandoned and Sinéad went on to produce her début album, 'The Lion And The Cobra', herself.

In the meantime she became pregnant by drummer John Reynolds and acquired a manager, Fachtna O'Ceallaigh.

The album was released to critical acclaim and impressive commercial success with sales of one million. A single, 'Mandinka', charted in the Top 20 and the album won a Grammy nomination and an appearance at the awards ceremony in Hollywood in February, 1989.

She released two other singles, one with outrageous New York feminist performance artist Karen Finley, and the other with New York rapper M.C. Lite.

'Nothing Compares 2U' was released in January, 1990, as a single and video. Both had immediate and massive impact. She shot to number one in Britain. Two months later the album, 'I Do Not Want What I Haven't Got' made the number one spot in the album charts immediately on release.

The single and the album went to number one in the American *Billboard* 100 singles and album charts within two weeks of each other.

A subsequent tour of America was a major success and was marked by her sweeping the MTV music video awards in September, 1990.

So there you have it, in a nutshell, so to speak, but how much wiser are you now about the girl who sheds a tear in 'Nothing Compares 2U' or screams 'You're a FUCKING LIAR' in 'Troy'? How much more do you know about the bovver-booted girl who sang at a 'Troops Out' rally in Dublin; who has sung at benefit concerts for Nelson Mandela and for AIDS research?

How much do you want to know about her and how much does she want you to know?

In one magazine article she was quoted as saying, "To me these records are like a chronological listing of every phase I've been through. I was 20 when I put out the first album and 15 when I wrote a lot of the songs. I was very fucked up and very unhappy. And that's how I remained until about six months before I started writing for the new one – which is simply a record about a 23-year-old human being and what she makes of her experiences.

"I don't have to reveal any more of my life than I want to, I don't have to spell it out for people, what business is it of theirs?" she snapped angrily in an Irish pub in November 1990.

It's one of those recurring Sinéad O'Connor paradoxes that she should make music entirely for herself yet, clearly, so many people want to listen.

She told *Rolling Stone* that her record company thought 'I Do Not Want What I Haven't Got' was too personal to put out. She herself wonders at people listening to songs like 'The Last Day Of Our Acquaintance' and why she wrote it and decides that's weird.

Yet just as young lovers have swooned to 'Moon River', pined to the strains of 'Only The Lonely', furied to the rage of 'God Save The Queen' and cried to the saccharine melodrama of Bobby Goldsboro's 'Honey', there are people somewhere and everywhere who believe today that some song was written just for them.

It's not just the singer. Not just the song. It's both of these and the listener that creates the magical relationship in music. None of these parties can remain aloof or detached.

No-one can expect an artist to assume responsibility for another person's perception but they know, just like the forlorn lover, what it means. People want to know about the singer who sings the song.

It's as simple as that. They want to understand the song and to do that they must understand the singer.

There is a hidden and cruel irony in public life stories – the more or the less you tell and reveal, the more people will want to know or imagine. That's why the lives of rock stars, movie stars and celebrities from any walk of life are no longer their own.

In a very short life and particularly in one hectic year, Sinéad O'Connor has realised the dream of a lonely 13-year-old girl, humming alone in a room full of old women, coughing and wheezing, to become a famous star. She has also begun to count the cost. Her life is lost in the myths of time.

Chapter Two

Colours Of Gold

Dublin is a small town, a very small town. Sinéad O'Connor's father, John, was my landlord for three years. It was a tiny, terraced two storey house in the old 'Liberties' part of the city. We were students, nurses and academics playing at being punks. It was a madhouse.

Every Thursday night John O'Connor, or more likely his wife, Viola, would turn up to collect the rent. They were patient, tolerant, good humoured people. They didn't have to be.

Viola O'Connor, née Suiter, is John O'Connor's second wife. His first marriage broke up in acrimony in the early seventies, close to Sinéad's eighth birthday. Viola Suiter is a quiet, intelligent and attractive woman. She wore a bemused expression that she may have saved for her visits to us. Her voice was soft and gentle and when she spoke, her Bangor County Down accent was preceded by a barely audible 'wee sigh'.

With Viola's three daughters, Jane, Lisa and Kate Suiter, the ranks of the O'Connor family were swelled to a total complement of eight, counting John O'Connor's five children by his first marriage – Joe, Eimear, John, Eoin and Sinéad.

John O'Connor is a healthy Dubliner with greying hair, a ruddy complexion and the same thick and curious arched eyebrows as his famous daughter. He has dark-ringed laughing eyes and his thin mouth is set in a permanent grin.

He enjoys a pint, a chat and a joke. A structural engineer by profession, he has also studied for, and been called to, the Bar of the Irish courts where his speciality is construction law. A grimly determined man, he once took off for a holiday to a Spanish resort with all his family about him and most of his study books as luggage. It is likely Sinéad inherited her own single-minded and stubborn nature from her father.

O'Connor once stood in my doorway on the day we were all leaving, resolutely determined to remain there until all outstanding bills had been settled. There was a party in full swing at the time and one student's father had arrived to help his son (who was in the throes of a nervous breakdown) remove his gear. John stayed. John got paid. He's a fair man.

O'Connor was raised in the same area of the city that he described in *The Sunday Tribune* of February 5, 1989 as "the independent republic of Francis Street." Nestled in the warren of narrow streets in the shadow of Dublin's only two Cathedrals, St. Patrick's and Christchurch, both Protestant, Francis Street is one of the key thoroughfares in the heart of the inner city Liberties.

Today, Francis Street is a curious mixture of the old and the new, the poor and the affluent. There are high priced antique shops, a gourmet restaurant that specialises in Russian and Scandinavian cuisine, a theatre that was once a music hall, then a cinema, then a bingo hall. Across the street stands the curious pillared edifice that is the Iveagh market, a unique covered street market. The colour and richness of the people and their language is as much a bargain as the oddball wares they peddle.

John O'Connor describes his own family as typical of the area. "Little reason, or none, was enough for them to make music," he wrote. His sister, Nell, sang in the chorus of the Dublin Grand Opera Society. His two brothers, Billy and Rory, are accomplished musicians, and his sister, Martha, "had a consummate knowledge of classical music and musicians."

Sinéad's mother, Marie, who died in a motor accident in 1985, was a tragic and disturbed figure. A dressmaker, she was a frequent member of the chorus in local productions of Gilbert and Sullivan comic operas and her father, who hailed from Waterford, had a love of Irish music and a sizeable collection of old records. She encouraged her children to explore their own musical talents. Sinéad and her sister, Eimear, were encouraged to sing. Sinéad's father, John, she has often remarked, has a fine tenor voice and a rich store of Irish ballads which he will sing at the slightest provocation.

John recalls walking with Sinéad and her sister Eimear up to the Hellfire Club on Dublin's Montpelier Hill that overlooks the city from the south side. He produced a business dictaphone, sat both girls on a rock by the side of the path and recorded them. "It was the first time I was stopped in my tracks by Sinéad's singing," he wrote in that *Sunday Tribune* article. She sang harmony with Eimear on 'Colours Of Gold' and solo on a song called 'Old Zip Coon'.

"I kept it on the tape," O'Connor told Mikal Gilmore of *Rolling Stone* in the summer of 1990. "It's interesting to hear how true Sinéad's voice was, even at that stage. She could hit a note on the head and hold it for 15 seconds or so – just like she can today."

There is no record of whether Sinéad's first sounds matched the passionate swooping howl that is so characteristic of her contemporary singing style. Singing was clearly a source of solace for her from an early age. "I remember when I was very young," she told *Rolling Stone*, "I'd go out for walks and I'd sort of be making little songs up. I think I was so fucked up that I wanted to make noises or something – like shout and scream about the whole thing."

She didn't, she says, set out with any notions of becoming a singer. "It was just that I could actually express the pain that I felt with my voice because I didn't have the facilities to express it in any other way. It was just all bubbling up in there and it had to come out."

She was born Sinéad Marie Bernadette O'Connor in the Cascia House nursing home at 13 Pembroke Street, Dublin on December 8, 1966. Her father described himself as a structural engineer on the birth certificate, and at the time he lived with his wife, Johanna Marie O'Connor (née O'Grady), at 10 Arnold Grove, Glenageary, Co. Dublin – a comfortable middle class suburb to the south of the city.

Sinéad was named after Sinéad Bean deValera, wife of the then President of Ireland, Eamon deValera, and the mother of the doctor who delivered her, Professor Eamon de Valera Jr. She was the midlechild of five, the others being Joseph, Eimear, John and Eoin in descending

"She could hit a note on the head and hold it for 15 seconds..."

JOHN O'CONNOR

Sinéad with her father, John O'Connor.

Sinéad, aged eight.

order of age.

John O'Connor remembers the day well. "Her brother Joe was three-years-old when Sinéad arrived and he went to evening mass with Kitty O'Grady, Sinéad's granny," he wrote. Young Joe created a commotion at the Mass as he wasn't offered any Communion. "Look at them eating it all up," he said, and later "Look at him locking it up and I got none."

Sinéad, John recalls, "was such a handy little size that I often carried her around under my arm."

The family, Roman Catholics, attended Mass that day as it was a Holy Day in the Catholic calendar and a very significant one since it celebrated the Immaculate Conception of Christ's mother, Mary, the Blessed Virgin, born without the 'Original Sin' that damns all Christians from birth. It is one of the most rigidly adhered to and fundamental tenets of the Roman Catholic church that Christ, the Son of God, was born of a Blessed Virgin Mother.

In Ireland it has even more significance, where Marian devotion is particularly fervent, and where fundamental religious beliefs have a strong effect on social mores and political creeds.

An understanding of a strong Irish Catholic upbringing is central to understanding Sinéad O'Connor and the powerful forces that have informed her life and education.

Sinéad's third name, Bernadette, is in recognition of St. Bernadette of Lourdes, in south west France, a key pilgrimage centre for Roman Catholics since the Virgin Mother appeared in a vision to a 14-year-old peasant girl, Bernadette, in 1858. Over three million people visit the shrine at Lourdes annually, bringing with them the incurably ill and crippled to bathe in the town's holy well.

Sinéad's mother, a devout Catholic, once took her to Lourdes. She told *Hot Press* in December 1989, "I don't think that I will ever again experience such intense emotional feelings as I did at Lourdes. It felt to me at the time like heaven." She recalls it as one of the "few truly happy moments of my childhood."

Sinéad told the same journalist that for much of her childhood she was obsessed with St. Bernadette and often believed herself to be the reincarnation of the Catholic saint.

Her strong religious beliefs helped her during the most turbulent years of her teens. During her worst days in a school for girls with behavioural problems in the north Dublin suburb of Drumcondra, she would lie awake at night praying for an apparition, wishing to be the next girl to see the Virgin Mary.

For a young Irish girl with such evocative middle names as Marie and Bernadette, who was steeped in an atmosphere of strong Catholic devotion, such imagery was powerful and often positive.

But there was a dark side too.

Chapter Three

Don't Cry For Me, Argentina

In 1966, the year Sinéad was born, Ireland celebrated the 50th anniversary of the 1916 Easter Rebellion, when a handful of Irish Republicans fought a bloody battle for the control of Dublin against the might of the British Imperial war machine.

Eamonn de Valera, one of the heroes of the insurrection, became President of Ireland for the second time in 1966, at the age of 83.

Admiral Nelson was blown off his pillar on Dublin's main thoroughfare, O'Connell Street, by an IRA bomb.

The Irish army moved in to remove the remaining 12-foot high stump and blew out every window in the street.

It was also the year that London became the centre of the 'swinging sixties' and to emphasise the country's all round superiority in matters that mattered, England also won the World Cup, beating the old enemy Germany in the final moments of extra time before a capacity crowd at Wembley Stadium. Myra Hindley and Ian Brady, the infamous Moors murderers, were sentenced to life imprisonment. A Catholic youth was shot dead in Northern Ireland.

Bob Dylan went electric when he appeared to a mixed reception in London's Albert Hall, booed by folk purists who shouted 'Judas' and cheered by rock fans. James Meredith, the first black student to brave the colour bar in the University of Mississippi in 1962, was shot in the back and legs when he entered Mississippi on a civil rights march. In South Africa, Prime Minister Dr Hendrik Verwoerd, the father of apartheid, was assassinated by a Bible quoting Parliamentary messenger.

One hundred and sixteen children and 28 adults were buried in an avalanche of slurry and coal slag that engulfed the Welsh mining village of Aberfan. Walt Disney, Buster Keaton and Montgomery Clift died, and the year's biggest hits were 'Distant Drums' by the dead country singer Jim Reeves, 'Strangers In The Night' by Frank Sinatra, and 'Spanish Flea' by Herb Alpert, a Mexicana-style trumpeter who would invest his earnings in his own record label called A&M Records, and sell it 23 years later to Polygram for 500 million dollars.

The swinging sixties, and all that was happening in the world outside her own home, meant little to Sinéad O'Connor, the conveniently sized baby bundle of energy that her father would occasionally carry under his arm like a log. She would come into consciousness during the seventies, a decade that seemed to bring her an unending barrage of misery and deep trauma. John and Marie O'Connor, who had married young, split up in 1975 when Sinéad was eight years of age. The split was bitter and acrimonious.

"There was a lot of fighting and aggression going on between my mother and father over a very long period and that quickly began to rub off on me," Sinéad told Liam Fay of *Hot Press*. "I felt very neglected and angry and no-one sat down and talked to me or asked how did I feel, so things just got worse."

Sinéad, Eimear and Joe went to live with their mother in Glenageary and while conditions there have been alluded to over the years, the truth about their existence remains unclear in a blur of omissions, denials and counter denials.Her father has acknowledged that Sinéad's time with her mother was by no means happy while Sinéad's own accounts of those years are carefully considered but never exaggerated.

She told *Melody Maker* journalist Paul Mathur, "My mother was sick but didn't realise it at first. I used to dread the way that tiny things would make her hit us, but at the same time, I really loved her. It was very strange … she would never let me out of the house to see boys and it got to the stage where I wouldn't even think before saying 'no' to any boy who asked me out."

Sinéad, aged seventeen.

"I wouldn't even think before saying 'no' to any boy who asked me out."

Sinéad would later refute this admission, claiming Mathur hadn't used a tape recorder and she had never said anything of the sort.

In a *Rolling Stone* interview Sinéad admitted life with her mother had been "extremely strict" and that she had been "severely abused". Her mother was ill, probably an alcoholic and dependent on prescribed anti-depressants such as Valium. She was also resentful of the disintegration of her own marriage, of the lost opportunities in her own life and of her ex-husband's pursuit of happiness elsewhere, in the arms of another.

This resentment was visited on her children and particularly the two girls, Sinéad and her sister, Eimear.Sinéad told *Rolling Stone*, "A child always thinks that it's their fault that these things happen. I was extremely fucked up about that for a long time. Between the family situation and Catholicism, I developed a real capacity for guilt."

Although Sinéad dedicated her first album, 'The Lion And The Cobra' to her mother, during that summer of 1984 she told a friend in Dublin how much she hated her mother who had abused and mistreated her and showed her nothing but contempt. Sinéad felt her mother's whole life had been a misery and that she had, in turn, made everyone else's life a misery too.

Nevertheless, her mother's sudden death in 1985 was an horrific shock to Sinéad. "I was completely and utterly destroyed," she told *Rolling Stone*.

"I felt that we had never really had a relationship. But now, looking back, I know that my mother knew I loved her very much and I know she loved me. More than anything, I just felt sorry for her."

Beatings were frequent and unannounced. They were brutal and cruel. "It could have been anything really. She was completely irrational. You know, like a button would be missing from my dress … somebody would be eating some peanuts or a spoon would be missing from a drawer or somebody's room would be untidy. I had a sock tied around a roller skate once and this really irritated her and she started to strike me," Sinéad recalled in the January, 1991 issue of *Esquire* magazine.

Sinéad and her sister Eimear were locked up in cupboards, naked, for days at a time, unfed and uncared for. They were struck with everything that was to hand – hockey sticks, carpet sweepers, her father's tennis racket.

Resistance brought even more severe retribution, so instead they learned to accept their punishment passively, "kneel on the floor and let her kick the shit out of me. If you'd put your arm up to protect yourself you were accused of trying to hit her back. So you didn't. You just knelt on the floor and had it done to you and then it was over until the next time," she recalled.

Her mother took them on shoplifting sprees and Sinéad often pretended to collect money for charity to have money to bring home to her mother.

During those years her father carried on a legal struggle to gain custody of his children from a legal system which, under the Irish constitution, provided cast iron custody protection for the maternal parent.

He became involved in the establishment of the Divorce Action Group, a wide-based pressure group formed to secure an amendment to the Irish constitution which specifically bans marital divorce in Ireland.

John O'Connor became Chairman and a prominent spokesman for the Divorce Action Group. The group gathered together many new forces of liberalism and pluralism in Ireland, as well as the hundreds of

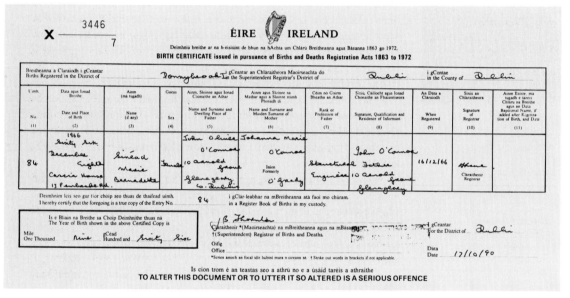

thousands of people whose lives were in ruins due to what they considered a legal anomaly, based on a selective and discriminatory religious moral teaching.

Aligned against them on the other side of the fence were the powerful forces of the Irish Catholic Moral Right – a fervently religious groundswell whose Catholic moral beliefs were considered even more fundamental than the words of the Irish Constitution, which in turn was considered an unshakable legal buttress of their beliefs.

In one bizarre episode John O'Connor argued the D.A.G. pro-amendment line on an Irish current affairs radio show while a 'Mrs O'Connor' counter-argued for a family solidarity fundamentalist group. Although John O'Connor was reluctant to point it out, the anti-amendment group had pulled a cruel irony on him. He was arguing against his estranged wife.

On a number of occasions Sinéad's mother was a patient at St. John of God's hospital which provided a therapeutic drugs and alcohol reha-

Sinéad O'Connor \ So Different

bilitation and 'drying out' programme. Her condition deteriorated as she developed incontinence and hair loss.

After the death of Marie O'Connor in a motor accident in 1985, Sinéad and her family cleared out some of her mother's belongings and found a large collection of tranquillisers like Mogadon and Valium, to which she had become addicted.

It was typical of a society with an extraordinary capacity for ignoring the truth even when it sits on its face, that Sinéad and her brothers and sister could be sent off to their Catholic, middle class schools, with bruises and black eyes and no-one 'noticed', no-one said anything.

Sinéad's mother was known as someone who would call the police if a football landed in her garden. On one occasion a neighbour did venture to phone the Irish Society For The Prevention Of Cruelty To Children, to report a suspected child beating in Sinéad's home.

Sinéad has said they wouldn't call because, she claimed, they said people in nice middle class areas like Arnold Grove in Glenageary weren't in the habit of beating up their children.

Sinéad's own detailed confession of these events in a magazine article earlier this year was prompted by her own anger at the hypocrisy that swept all pain and ill treatment under the carpet. In a characteristically frank, brutal and brave interview, she decided it was her duty to speak out when others would choose to be silent.

In 1979 Sinéad walked out on her mother and went to live with her father who had by then remarried and turned to study law. She later told friends about her bizarre relationship with her mother who, in the aftermath of the break-up of her marriage, had become devoutly religious to the point of fanaticism. She deeply resented her ex-husband's new life with Viola Suiter.

Sinéad was attending Sion Hill junior school."She was a tomboy and her circle of friends, more like a gang in fact, were nearly all male," recalls Kevin O'Byrne, a school pal from those days and later a member of Ton Ton Macoute, her first band.

"At that time she had a reputation for being a nutter and she was famous for her exhibitionist stunts. She'd been barred from Stillorgan bowling alley for wearing tampons in her hair. She revelled in that sort of thing – being provocative, offending people's sensibilities."

Sinéad's wild behaviour in those days went even further. She became a regular truant, hanging out in the same Stillorgan bowling alley, playing video games hour after hour when she should have been in school.

She also began a brief career as a petty thief and shoplifter. "I stole money from my parents and then I progressed to stealing money from other people," she once said. Soon she was stealing regularly. "I very quickly became addicted to shoplifting – I didn't steal very big things but I stole a lot of small things, clothes, sweets, perfume."

Her father realised she was heading for big trouble if she continued in this way. "She never did anything seriously wrong," he later said. "She wasn't a sex fiend or a dope fiend. But after she got caught nicking a pair of shoes in a shop in downtown Dublin, there was a fear that she was getting wayward."

Sinéad's behaviour was directly related to the turmoil of her domestic situation. "I don't really know what effect it had on me," she told Irish teen magazine *Fresh*. "It obviously frightened me because I didn't under-

> *"I stole a lot of small things, clothes, sweets, perfume."*

stand at all what was happening and I was too young to ask someone to sit down and explain it to me. To tell you the truth, I didn't really think about the effect it had on me."

Her father felt a sense of guilt from the whole affair. "She had good bloody reason to be unhappy with her home life," he told *Rolling Stone*, "though maybe it's my own feeling of guilt – my failure to do what was right for the kids at the time – that's speaking here."

Sinéad's truant episodes were not without their humour. When she was nine and attending Alexandra College in Milltown, Dublin, she often joined her step-sister Lisa in the nearby local primary school, posing as a "friend on holiday from England" and joining in the class until her absence from Alexandra was remarked upon.

Meanwhile John O'Connor was trying to sustain his business interests while pursuing a new career in law as a barrister. He was also still a prime mover in the campaign to reform the Irish constitution and remove the ban on divorce that had led to thousands of people living in anomalous, unhappy and legally ambivalent relationships with partners they loved but could not marry under the law of the State.

Sinéad was not expelled from Sion Hill, according to the authorities there. She was moved from the school, though, following discussions between her father and the Principal. "We had a very happy relationship with Sinéad at Sion Hill. She was a very gentle girl," the school Principal told me, smarting at earlier inaccurate accounts such as that in *Rolling Stone*, June 14, 1990, which described the school – an average convent-run secondary level school – as "a school for girls with behavioural problems, run by Dominican nuns." "We recommended and arranged her transfer in consultation with her father," said the Principal. "What was going on had nothing to do with Sinéad."

The O'Connor residence at 10 Arnold Grove, Glenageary.

Sinéad O'Connor \ So Different

Sinéad's next port of call was Grianan Training Centre, a gloomy edifice of no clearly discernible architectural age, run by the Sisters of Our Lady of Charity for the Eastern Health Board. There may have been a brief stint in Glengara Park, a posh Church of Ireland boarding school on Dun Laoghaire's Lower Glenageary Road. This has since closed, the land developed with luxury private housing and the school converted to a private nursing home. Sinéad left Sion Hill in 1981.

The only mention of Glengara Park is made by her father who recounts an amusing tale when writing about Sinéad in the *Sunday Tribune*. "One day, Sinéad, Eimear, John and myself passed the (Protestant) church (near Glengara Park) on a walk. The verger recognised the two girls and invited them in to say, 'a little prayer'." He then asked them to sing a hymn and they duly obliged and sang the Lourdes' hymn, 'The Bells Of The Angelus'.

In 1982, the records show her transfer to Grianan, a training centre for girls with behavioural problems on Dublin's northside suburb of Drumcondra. She was also enrolled in the local secondary school, Maryfield College, also on Grace Park Road in Drumcondra and also run by the Sisters of Our Lady of Charity.

Her stay there has often been described, particularly by Sinéad and later distorted in magazine and newspaper reports, as a sort of jail term.

This was the only 'reform' type institution Sinéad ever attended. She joined the Training Centre in 1982 and left in 1983. It was a voluntary visit, in so much as she had not been ordered there by any court, juvenile or otherwise. She didn't like it there but for all its Dickensian grimness it was to prove a vital turning point in her life.

Sinéad, aged seventeen.

Evergreen

"I have never – and I probably will never – experience such panic and terror and agony over anything. If you were bad they sent you upstairs to sleep in the old folks' home. You'd be there in the pitch black. You can smell the shit and the puke and everything and these old women are moaning in their sleep."

This was how Sinéad recalled life at Grianan to Pat Lambert in her first ever interview with *Rolling Stone* in April, 1988.

Grianan's 'inmates', for the want of a better word, were for the most part young women with disturbed family or social backgrounds. Many had been institutionalised from an early age – put up for adoption or fostered from their homes. Others had been involved in the same kind of petty crime and truancy that had led Sinéad's father to place her there.

Attached to the training centre, then in the same building though with separate entrances, was an old folks' home populated largely by ageing spinsters, a throwback to the era when younger daughters from rural families were sent away to a convent when suitable husbands and appropriate dowries were thin on the ground.

Jeannette Byrne was a psychology student at University College, Dublin (UCD). Her uncle, Father Patrick Byrne, was a Marist priest, Principal of Chanel College boys' secondary school in another nearby Dublin suburb of Coolock.Father Byrne was an educational psychologist and had associations with many of the Eastern Health Board's training centres like Grianan. He gave Jeannette a list of likely centres to which she might usefully apply to perform voluntary work and gain valuable clinical experience. One of those was Grianan and Jeannette became a visitor and volunteer worker at the centre.

"My interests were more in the line of education and drama, particularly with younger people and I was asked to do some part time work with the unit in the evenings," Jeannette recalls. "I was already teaching music and guitar, just to really be there with the girls as a visitor and general helper, so I was there on a more semi-permanent basis than I used to be, and I filled in for members of staff on their holidays.

"It was on one of those days Sinéad came to see the unit which was normal procedure for the girls. She came to be introduced to everybody and have a look around and a few weeks later she moved in."

Jeannette vividly recalls Sinéad's first day at the Centre. "She was very striking, very black hair, she was quite heavily made up but very unusually – which was probably the last time she was ever that made up."

Sinéad was 15 at the time.

It was clear from the start that Sinéad was something special. "If you met her at that time," Jeannette recalls, "she had gone through a lot of trauma and she was able to get herself above it and in fact she used all that trauma to her own benefit … she has great strength, she wasn't going to let it get her down, whereas many children can't cope, she was well able to cope, she knew where it was at …"

Sinéad was a popular girl in the centre. She attended the local convent school and was not in need of any special classes. She was "incredibly bright" and many of the other girls, more accustomed to the rigours of institutional life, were charmed by her charisma and looked up to her.

Sinéad was no slouch at asserting her own individuality. "I remember her going off in uniform," says Jeannette. "I think it was quite long and I think having to conform in the uniform didn't appeal to her, she was always doing something individual to the clothes."

Clothes weren't the only matters with which Sinéad had difficulty conforming. "I suppose she thought some of the rules were stupid, but the rules were there for everybody and without them there would have been no structure. A lot of the girls hadn't any sort of structure in their lives so they provided reassurance."

Sinéad's term there was also an exam year for her. In the secondary or high school level of the Irish educational system students are required to sit for their Intermediate Certificate. Sinéad was seen as a bright but sometimes lazy or uncommitted student.

She excelled in English, particularly in creative essay writing where her powers of imagination came into their own. Her former English teacher, Mrs Nuala O'Connor, now Vice Principal at Maryfield College, remembers her as a very quiet girl in class but one with strong opinions and feelings about social issues. "She wouldn't follow the convention, she had a mind of her own," Mrs O'Connor recalls.

By coincidence Mrs O'Connor discovered late in Sinéad's year at Maryfield that she was indirectly related to her by marriage. Mrs O'Connor's husband was Sinéad's father's first cousin.

That year Shakespeare's *Merchant Of Venice* was required reading for the Intermediate Certificate English course, and its compelling theme of justice served struck a chord with Sinéad.

"She was an upholder of the downtrodden," says Mrs O'Connor. "She wrote me an essay once about an old-down-and-out woman – she would chose the most interesting subjects to write about – and she had very strong feelings about some things, social issues and people who weren't getting a fair crack of the whip."

In the Grianan centre Sinéad was even less inclined to toe the line and occasionally she was sent to the dormitory to sleep with the older people as punishment, a terrifying prospect for an impressionable teenager with a vivid imagination.

She was also developing an interest in music and guitar playing and was showing an aptitude for it. "She had a natural ability," Jeannette Byrne remembers. Jeannette taught rudimentary guitar classes and organised the girls into a group to sing at staff weddings as well as at special schools for handicapped children. They also put on a show once or twice a year for the old women in Grianan and for visitors.

Grianan's Principal, Sr. Margaret Fogarty, also recognised Sinéad's special talents and encouraged Jeannette to spend a little more time with her. At one stage Sinéad was taken to town with Jeannette to buy a new

"She was very striking, very black hair, quite heavily made up but very unusually."

JEANNETTE BYRNE

guitar for her. "I went out with her with a good sum of money after Christmas to buy her a guitar. She was already writing songs at that stage."

Sinéad would join in the school carol singing and many evenings ended in sing-songs and sessions. "Sinéad would do her party piece, 'Don't Cry for Me, Argentina' which was much requested by the Principal who loved Sinéad's very haunting, very pure voice. We used to have competitions between us as to who could hold a note, she always beat me and held her last note and just kept on going ..."

Jeannette's fiancé would often call at the centre to pick her up in the evening. He began playing Bob Dylan songs for the girls. "He was really into Dylan and I had a lot of Dylan songbooks and he and Sinéad used to sing 'Hurricane' for the girls. He got Sinéad into stronger rock chords which is something I didn't do at all, I was more for softer accompaniment and ballads and I was stronger on the singing side."

Jeannette was married the following March, 1983. "I always said I'd have the girls to sing and so I asked her to do a solo. I wasn't having hymns or a straight conventional ceremony. I wanted different pieces of music so I asked her to sing 'Evergreen', which she sang beautifully and that's where she was heard by Paul, my brother, and his band, In Tua Nua. When I went off for my honeymoon for a week they phoned the centre and asked the Principal if Sinéad could go and do some work with them and the rest is history ..."

Take My Hand

"She was the lead voice in the choir, she sang 'Evergreen' at the rehearsal for the wedding and I was just blown out," recalls Paul Byrne, Jeannette Byrne's brother and drummer with nascent Irish rock combo, In Tua Nua.

It was a time when Dublin was beginning to buzz with music again, following the success of U2 whose persistent efforts now began to reap tangible rewards. There was a pervasive air of optimism, as though their success might reflect on anyone who was brave enough to follow in their footsteps.

In Tua Nua was in its infancy at that stage. They had made no clear decision to form a group but each member of the small group of friends was working towards the idea – writing songs and music and recording rough demos. They were encouraged in their efforts by U2's Bono who was a friend of fiddle player Steve Wickham and uileann piper Vinnie Kilduff. Both Wickham (later to join The Waterboys and now with The Texas Kellys, a Tex-Mex and bluegrass band that includes Paul Byrne on drums) and Kilduff had toured with U2 while Kilduff had played on the second U2 album, 'October' and Wickham featured on the third, 'War'.

"Martin Clancy had written a track and I had written a track and we were just trying to get In Tua Nua together.

"There were millions of musicians and no-one really knew quite what was going on, this was when it was just music, no songs … loads of tracks and just jamming. So Ivan (their guitarist) gave his piece to Leslie (Dowdall, In Tua Nua's lead singer) because she was recording in Eamonn Andrews' studios where Ivan was working and Martin had nobody to sing on his track. It was just the week we had been in Westland studios and we had a 24-track recording that sounded brilliant, so I asked Sinéad if she would like to do some work on it … so myself and Martin went up to see her that night at the school and we gave her the tape."

The following morning Sinéad was scheduled to sit her 'mock inter', a sort of dress rehearsal for the State exam that was three months away.

"I didn't expect anything from her for another week but the next evening she rang … she had everything, lyrics, melody, arrangement … everything worked out to a tee, so we drove up to her and she wanted to play it to us … it was perfect. It was 'Take My Hand'. It was a fast song then and when we recorded it later for Island, Steve Cooney (producer) slowed it all down … but it was fast … we were just blown out by it."

Byrne and Clancy contacted Sister Margaret, Grianan's Principal, and asked if they could borrow Sinéad for a recording session. She agreed.

"We went in at the weekend and demoed it. We demoed her vocal on the four-track to see how it sounded and we booked studio time the next week … I remember I had to borrow a friend's car and get her from the school to the studio and back, and the car was an uninsured banger. That very evening we all sat down and decided to form a band. It was her second time in a studio and she took to it like a fish to water."

Sinéad's school holiday occurred shortly afterwards and all that summer was spent in and out of Eamonn Andrews' studio in Dublin's Harcourt Street. "We were all more or less living in there because Ivan was working there, so we used to go in there at night and mess around."

Sinéad wanted to join the band. "We were saying 'Sinéad, you have to go back to school', we were all into taking this seriously, we were all giving up college, we were all about 20 or 21 and Sinéad was 15 so we said, 'Sinéad, it's not on.' She was really enthusiastic and she couldn't understand why she couldn't be in the band."

Sinéad, aged nineteen.

TO REORDER YOUR UPS DIRECT THERMAL LABELS:

1. Access our supply ordering website at **UPS.COM**® or contact UPS at 800-877-8652

2. Please refer to Label # 01774006 when ordering.

Shipper agrees to the UPS Terms and Conditions of Carriage/Service found at www.ups.com and at UPS service centers. If carriage includes an ultimate destination or stop in a country other than the country of departure, the Convention on the Unification of Certain Rules Relating to International Transportation By Air as amended (Warsaw Convention) or the Montreal Convention may apply and in most cases limits UPS's liability for loss or damage to cargo. Shipments transported partly or solely by road into or from a country that is party to the Convention on the Contract for the International Carriage of Goods By Road (CMR) are subject to the provisions in the CMR notwithstanding any clause to the contrary in the UPS Terms. Except as otherwise governed by such international conventions or other mandatory law, the UPS terms limit UPS's liability for damage, loss or delay of this shipment. There are no stopping places which are agreed upon at the time of tender of the shipment and UPS reserves the right to route the shipment in any way it deems appropriate.

01774006   RRD

B0236

MFM-2021-00236-B0236

UsedVeryGood

Sinead O'Connor: So Different

Paul Byrne still shakes his head in amazement when he recalls how fast she put 'Take my Hand' together. "I've been in bands for years and I gave this girl a backing track and she had lyrics, melody and structure all organised that night while doing her exams. I've been in bands where you could wait six months for a singer to come up with songs. We all knew Sinéad had it but we all felt you couldn't have a band with a 15-year-old."

In Tua Nua already had a singer, anyway; Leslie Dowdall, whose voice has often been compared with the folkiness of Sandy Denny and the power of Grace Slick. "We were looking at two singers and they were both very good in different ways. Sinéad had a very pure, clean voice and Leslie had this big rocking voice. The band was split in two directions anyway, half rock and half folky and acoustic, we decided we wanted to play live so we went for the rock. It was that simple at the time. We dropped her and she didn't take it brilliantly, she was pretty upset … we didn't see her for a good while after that. She went off to school for a year and then we met up again and there was a distance there … but she was a kid when this was happening and that year when she came back she was an adult … something must have happened, she was more assertive."

Twelve months later In Tua Nua had signed to Island Records following the local success of their début single, 'Coming Thru', the first release on the fledgling U2-owned Mother Records label which had been set up to help young Irish bands with short-term single release contracts.

"We were doing our début EP with Steve Cooney," says Paul Byrne. "We were going through all the material that we had demoed since we signed to Island and then he says, 'Is there anything else?' and we said 'There's some stuff we did before we signed.' We let him hear it and he heard 'Take My Hand' and he says, 'That's your best song', and we said, 'Fine'. We got in touch with Sinéad and organised the copyright and everything … I've heard since that she preferred the original fast version."

Sinéad's recollection, three years later in a *Melody Maker* interview, was slightly different, understandably shrugging off the rejection for other reasons. "I was doing school exams at the time so I couldn't join the band … it was only after that that I decided to become a professional singer."

"She had lyrics, melody and structure all organised that night while doing her exams. I've been in bands where you could wait six months for a singer to come up with songs."

PAUL BYRNE

Drink Before The War

Her rejection by In Tua Nua strengthened Sinéad's resolve to pursue a musical career. She had found a focus for her own individual creative energies. She was 15 and already she had been introduced to the magic of a recording studio. People clearly liked her voice, she had begun to write songs and she had performed and recorded one of those with a band.

Her father's decision to send her to Newtown School in Waterford, an exclusive, £3,000 a year, 200-year-old Quaker boarding school in the south coast port town of Waterford, was probably an effort to have Sinéad finish her secondary education outside the constraints of conventional Irish convent education.

It was her second boarding school but that's where the comparison with Grianan began and ended.

Newtown School is known in Waterford by local people as 'the blue school', a euphemism for 'Protestant school' and there is a perception of it as a school for the well heeled Protestant Anglo-Irish, the children of foreign dignitaries, either resident in Ireland or seeking an English-speaking school that will furnish their children with the wherewithal for resourcefulness and social etiquette in the big bad world. These days many of the children in the school are from Catholic homes, mostly middle class and professional.

The school is run by the teachers and the general atmosphere is informal and friendly. It is co-educational and interdenominational. Students can acquire passes to go to worship in any of the town's churches at weekends. Many of them, whether they are Methodists, Baptists, Presbyterians, Church of Ireland or Roman Catholic, gather in the local Catholic church – it's the nearest.

Sinéad must have suffered culture shock in her new environment – someone who had thrived on kicking against the system must have been bewildered to find nothing to kick against. She had spent most of her school life in convent schools. "With Catholic education," she told *Melody Maker*'s Helen Fitzgerald, "if you mentioned the word 'tampon' you'd get expelled." An outrageous exaggeration, but she was lashing out at the repressive guilt-ridden regime that pervaded a convent education, particularly for girls.

"Nuns are all very well," she stormed, "but they've never had a lay in their lives so I don't really think they're in any position to counsel people about such things. In Ireland you just can't escape from religion, it follows you everywhere and of course if you speak your mind you're the Devil Incarnate."

Sinéad's education, like most young Irish people, was largely conducted by religious Orders – Christian Brothers, priests and nuns. For Sinéad the nuns practised their own peculiar brand of psychological violence – imposing notions of guilt, sin and repression on her in their efforts to straighten her wayward habits. But trying to break the spirit of the iron-willed O'Connor was nigh on impossible – she was Cool Hand Sinéad fighting the 'walkin' boss'.

Her impressions of the nuns and her Catholic upbringing have been coloured by time, her mother and her own imagination. "The religion there (Ireland) is riddled with hypocrisy," she has said. "Illegitimacy is still so shameful and lots of country girls go through agonies of guilt because they're not allowed contraception or abortion, yet there are priests out there having affairs with women – and I'll bet their girlfriends are on the pill."

But her metaphorical polemics, while they hold some shade of truth in a country where Catholicism is such an intrinsic part of the body politic as to flavour ideologies, have been invested with far more meaning by English and American journalists inclined to believe what she says in a more literal fashion.

Sinéad bitterly resented her 'incarceration' in the Grianan training unit. "I was very bitter about it for a long time," she told *Hot Press* in 1989. "In retrospect, I see that I had to learn certain things and those places did teach me that there were ways of behaving and ways of not behaving. I deserved it because I hadn't been giving my parents a very easy time. In the long run I think it was a good experience because I met a lot of good people and learnt a lot of important things ..."

The most important aim was clearly to prevent her from stealing and perhaps, in her own estimation, to steer her away from more serious offences. Looking back at it she believes her father had no choice other than to send her away, in the absence of any real understanding of why a girl like her should misbehave so badly.

Painful as the decision to send her away was for her father, it was obviously the right one. "(It) gave her new strengths of self-sufficiency and independence," he wrote. "Sinéad didn't like it very much and refers to it as if she had been incarcerated there. However, the same school and the modern methods of self-awareness it taught were helpful to Sinéad."

Sinéad later told a friend how she had hated 'reform' school – locals in the Drumcondra area of Dublin refer to it as the 'school for naughty girls' – and how her parents had sent her there 'for her own good'. She confided that the stay there had probably done her some good but the regime was too strict and that her parents had eventually relented to her pleas and agreed to take her out, on condition that she went to a boarding school.

Sinéad arrived in Newtown School in Waterford in the Autumn of 1983. She was quick to assert her own independence and individuality.

Her step-sister, Jane Suiter, had already been to the school. Assessments of Jane, by people who were around at the time, range from 'wild child' to 'right bitch' and her image, to say the least, helped to colour people's expectations and perceptions of the latest member of her family to arrive at the school.

Sinéad, though quiet, struck up a friendship with Gaelic teacher Joe Falvey. Falvey had an interest in music going back to his own days as a student in Cork City where he ran a small club that is now Sir Henry's, one of the city's most happening live music venues.

Sinéad O'Connor \ Drink Before The War

Falvey, stocky and hirsute, has a grey flecked full beard covering a round, ruddy complexion and mischievous, twinkling eyes. A married man, in his late thirties, he has worked all his life in Newtown and takes an active interest in all the school's activities. He always took on the task of organising the autumn mid-term supper dance.

Less than four weeks after arriving at the school, Sinéad instigated the establishment of a Student Council in one of those periodic outbreaks of democracy that occur in schools.

"She offered to come into town with me to buy decorations for the dance. We began to chat and she said how much she liked the school, what a change it was and how she was determined to establish her own identity and to be known as Sinéad O'Connor as opposed to somebody's sister."

Sinéad threw herself into becoming involved with the dance and the organisation of the music. Shortly afterwards Falvey came across Sinéad singing and playing guitar in the school hall. "I've been here since 1972 and there have been very few pupils in that time that you'd come across singing and playing the way teenagers do, so I was even more surprised when I was passing the school hall to hear the sound of a guitar and someone singing. There was a bunch of teenagers huddled around the player and when I looked it was Sinéad.

"That was about October 1983 and she was into folk songs, like Bob Dylan songs. I remember her asking 'Would you like to hear one of the songs I have written myself?' and I said , 'Oh surely', and I was impressed. Here she was 16-years-old, she had this very strong voice. The songs were belted out and there was a striking urgency about the style of the music. But it was the maturity of her lyrics more than any-thing else that stood out. I had to keep reminding myself that this was a 16-year-old – people of that age are often very uncertain in the expres-sion of their feelings but she showed extraordinary insights."

Sinéad, he remembers, was a lively and fun loving girl in Newtown, a sharp contrast to the more introverted and quiet girl at Maryfield College. "It may sound like a cliché but she was popular and she had lots of friends here … she was always part of any bit of crack that was going on since she had a sense of a bit of fun."

She was also a prankster and usually in the thick of any 'devilment' that was happening, like a midnight feast or a foray over the walls into the town.

"I think the turning point in that particular phase of her time here and her evolution as a singer and performer was sparked off by news of a competition from the Tipperary Peace Festival. They had circulated the schools looking for young people who might write and perform a peace song for the festival. She brought this piece of paper up to me and said, 'What do you think, sir, should I enter?' 'Well, Sinéad,' I said, 'if you are to, let's go about it in a professional way, why not get a few of your songs recorded?"

Falvey contacted Brian O'Reilly, the brother of an old friend of his and the moving force behind a local jazz rock combo, Loudest Whisper. O'Reilly owned his own recording studio, Fiona Studios in Fermoy, Co. Cork."He told me he had a student who wanted to make a demo tape and he arranged a time and date for a three-hour session," says O'Reilly.

Joe rang his brother, Noel, a keyboard player, and arranged to meet him in Fermoy and Sinéad, Joe Falvey and Jeremy Scott-Naber, a friend of Sinéad's who often accompanied her in their school sessions, set off in Joe's car across the hills to Fermoy.

"We pooled our resources. I supplied the car and the petrol while the cost of the recording was going to be £50 and Jeremy and Sinéad paid half of that each. It was relatively cheap when you consider the enormous cost of recording studios, but one, it was being done as a favour and two, it wasn't as if it was a band so it was more straight forward," says Joe.

"So we met with my brother Noel, had a cup of coffee and headed off to the studio. It was during that recording session, when we did four songs in three hours, that I first got a real insight into the potential of Sinéad and the talent that she had."

Sinéad had not wasted her time in those summer days with In Tua Nua during 1983 in Eamonn Andrews' Studios in Dublin. A quick learner, she had grasped the essentials of studio technique; while hanging around making coffee, she was looking, listening and learning.

"Here she was with a very experienced producer, at 16 with a very clear-cut idea about the way she wanted the songs done, the way she wanted them recorded, the sound effects she wanted. The fact that we got four songs done in three hours was due to the fact that she had obviously very clearly thought out in advance what she wanted.

"I can still remember Brian O'Reilly looking at this young one with astonishment," says Joe Falvey.

"She was popular and had lots of friends here... she was always part of any bit of crack that was going on..."

JOE FALVEY

He had mentioned having a celebratory drink after the recording session before the long drive back over the hills to Waterford, but Sinéad and Jeremy were both on a high and wanted to get back to Waterford as soon as possible.

It was a dark and wet winter's night and the road from Fermoy to Waterford was a narrow mountain highway with more turns than a corkscrew. "I will always remember it," says Joe. "That four-track demo was nearly worn out by the time we got back at midnight. A couple of copies of the tape were made and for the next couple of days everyone was going round looking for a copy of 'the tape' to play on their cassette players. She was a kind of a superstar in the school for a few days."

Sinéad later gave the master of the demo tape to Joe Falvey shortly before 'one of her departures'."I still have it, it's a treasure," he says.

The song Sinéad wrote for the Peace Festival in Tipperary was 'Drink Before The War'. The other tracks on the tape were 'Just Like U Said It Would B', another original that later made its way onto 'The Lion And The Cobra' and two covers, one an old folk ballad, 'Black Is The Colour' and a Bob Dylan cover, 'Simple Twist Of Fate'.

The Peace Festival and the song writing competition were promptly forgotten in the euphoria of the recording session and its results. "I had various friends in town who ran an arts club in T&H Dolan's (a local pub)," recalls Joe Falvey. "I told the club secretary at the time there was a girl in the school who I thought had a lot of talent and he obliged me by giving her a support slot there one night. Most of the audience had come to see the main act of the evening that I now can't remember, nor can anybody else." Joe sat listening to Sinéad with her boyfriend, Craig Johnson. Jeremy Maber accompanied her on guitar. There was a good crowd of 100 to 120 in the tiny club at the back of the pub and support acts in T&H were usually treated with light humoured indulgence.

"I can still remember it graphically," Joe says. "They were stunned. Sinéad began to sing and they saw this girl on the stage and there was a stunned silence that one so little could have such a powerful voice. The intensity with which she sang and this great soulful roar which is characteristic of some of her songs – it overwhelmed the audience there – you could hear a pin drop for the next three quarters of an hour. It was really at that moment I said, 'My God, that girl has an incredible talent'."

Sinéad may have even played a support slot there for someone she later identified as her hero and role model, Irish folk singer Christy Moore. She has often attributed the startling vocal volumes she can achieve to having to shout to be heard in a noisy pub atmosphere.

Falvey felt the recording and the début performance triggered something in Sinéad and she began to take her career into her own hands. She made her own contacts in the Waterford clubs and set up gigs for herself and Jeremy Maber. They were calling themselves 'Sive' after a popular play by Irish playwright, John B. Keane.

Fired by enthusiasm and a new self assurance she even approached a local pirate radio station, WLR and persuaded them to interview her.

Earlier during that summer of 1984 Sinéad placed an ad in the 'Musicians Wanted' classified section in *Hot Press* magazine. It led to her meeting Columb Farrelly, a musician and songwriter in his late twenties who harboured ambitions of finding the perfect female voice for his songs.

> *"It was as if Sinéad was not responsible for the noise that came out of her mouth."*
> COLUMB FARRELLY

Ton Ton Macoute leader Columb Farrelly.

Farrelly had travelled extensively, lived rough and worked in numerous odd jobs. He had a fascination for 'musical archaeology' and exploring the Arabic roots in traditional Irish music. His own music leaned towards a fusion of Caribbean rhythms, Arabic vocal styles and arcane lyrics. He was also a student of occult theories although he shrugs off such associations now as 'dabbling and party tricks'.

"One May afternoon in 1984 I was sitting in a small office in the back of one of those gloomy Georgian houses, on the shadowy side of Upper Mount Street near the Pepper Cannister church," he recalls.

"I had all but given up on trying to find a suitable female voice to interpret my songs. The nearest I'd come was a woman called Val, a real belter but our potential partnership had come to a sudden end when her mother, the actress Brenda Dowling, was accidentally killed by a motor cyclist and shortly afterwards Val moved to Hollywood.

"So there I was idling over the 'Musicians Wanted' column in a half interested way when I was struck by an idea. I had always been interested in 'dowsing' (divining) so I decided it might be interesting to experiment. Attached to my key ring there was a sort of spherical imitation crystal, a cheap bauble really, but it served the purpose. Dangling this makeshift pendulum over the 'Musicians Wanted' column I gave it a little swing forward as proscribed to start it off. After some time the bauble ceased its swinging motion and began to take up a circular one. If I was consciously causing this thing to happen then it only goes to demonstrate the power of suggestion. The thing was spinning on an ad that read something like ... 'FEMALE SINGER seeks band, Call Sinéad. XXXXXX. No messers'." Farrelly decided to ring the number.

"The voice of an elderly man answered the phone. When I asked if I could speak to Sinéad I was subjected to a stream of invective. Apparently *Hot Press* had misprinted the number and I was at least the tenth caller that day. I rang *Hot Press* and after some persuasion the girl in the advertising department looked up the classified ads file and came up with the correct number."

Sinéad answered the phone. The first thing Farrelly remembers was the quality of her voice. "It had an attractive blurry tone, her accent was quite definitely southside." They chatted and agreed to meet. He made a show of having to flick through his empty diary to 'find a window'; she was nonchalant and alluded to 'many other callers'. No mention was made of the wrong number in the *Hot Press* ad.

One hour later Sinéad was on Columb Farrelly's doorstep dressed in jeans and a T-shirt, her collar-length hair tousled and a guitar slung over her shoulder. She sang a Bob Dylan song for him. An hour later, he recalls, he was convinced she had ... "The combination of a star on her forehead and a fire in her belly to make it." All she needed, he believed, was her nose pointed in the right direction. Over the next couple of weeks they set about assembling a band.

Chapter Seven

VuDu 4U

"I put this ad in Hot Press and found this weird bass player guy who wanted to form a band. We found a conga player and a drummer and did quite well on the Irish college circuit … I was singing all his songs, though, and I didn't realise for a while how weird this guy was. He was into voodoo and witchcraft. Some of his songs were brilliant but eventually I was advised to leave the band. Things got pretty unpleasant and I wanted to perform my own songs anyway," Sinéad told Helen Fitzgerald in *Melody Maker* in April, 1986.

History has not been kind to Ton Ton Macoute, the band assembled by Sinéad and Columb Farrelly that summer of 1984.

Repeated reports that Sinéad was 'unhappy' with Ton Ton Macoute and had no fond memories of her year with them caused dismay among the ranks of the band. From 1986 onwards, as more and more interviews with the new rising star Sinéad O'Connor appeared in music magazines, so did the put-downs of her old band mates. They even lost a string of bookings.

Nigel Grainge of Ensign Records told *Rolling Stone*, "They looked like another god-awful pub rock band."

In what was perhaps a more honest assessment of her time with the band and her reason for leaving them, she told Molly McAnailly Burke of *Hot Press*, "It got too heavy after a while and wasn't fun for me any more. We started arguing and soon I just wanted to go off and do my own thing – I just wasn't enjoying myself. Their reasons for being musicians and mine were very different – Columb wants to put forward his views of the world in a way which respect in some ways and disrespect in others. He's into witchcraft and that completely freaked me out. I'm a singer who likes to have a laugh, to say what I want to say in a nice way, to have fun, to use my talents to please people."

Columb Farrelly has been given a vaguely shadowy image – that of a manipulative and paranoid Svengali, holed up in some dusty attic, dabbling in arcane and esoteric religions and sciences and informing the world of his intents and activities with press releases and despatches, delivered by his assorted acolytes and minions. The band's later association with Irish psychic Zak Martin has probably accounted for some of this – they even featured a song based on Zak's annual predictions which included a portent of the American bombing of Tripoli, four months before the event, not to mention the destruction of a certain well known wall in middle Europe!

Farrelly, a former film stunt man who now works in film soundtrack composition, dismisses rumours of paranoia, witchcraft and manipulation with a dismissive shrug. There was a time, he says, when he would have got annoyed about it but it's too late to stop it now, he sighs with resignation. To this day he is unsure why Sinéad O'Connor turned on the band and continues to revile them in interviews with magazines.

Their collaboration from the summer of 1984 to the following March, 1985, was fruitful. Farrelly had interesting ideas about music, the fusion of melodies and the use of an Arabic scale in singing which have since become distinctive trademarks of Sinéad O'Connor. She gained valuable stage experience with a band. In addition Farrelly did hold a store of 'knowledge' of those esoteric sciences drawn from his self-styled 'shelf of paperback wisdom'.

Although denying or belittling the influence of magic or witchcraft in the band's activities for reasons of his own, Farrelly did use Ton Ton Macoute as a vehicle to promote his own quest for power and influence.

During the few weeks after their first meeting Sinéad and Columb met regularly at her father's house in Merton Park, Ranelagh, a fashionable Dublin suburb.

"Sinéad seemed almost ravenous for melodies. No sooner had I croaked out a melodic idea to her, she would swallow it wholesale and regurgitate it back at me with such a passion that when the last note died away we would both be left grinning at each other, breathlessly," is his colourful reflection of those days.

"It was as if Sinéad was not entirely responsible for the noise that came out of her mouth," he says today. "It was one of those 'this-thing-is-bigger-than-both-of-us' feelings, almost unholy."

Farrelly's age and travelling experiences lit something in Sinéad who was eager, young and gullible enough to find Columb exotic and fascinating. "I've always had a deep interest in what now has become 'world music'. At that time I was into Rumanian, Bulgarian, Indian, North African and what have you. We spent quite a bit of time with her voice scatting my guitar lines, trying Arabic scales. Sinéad really resonated with this. We both enthused over the connections between Arabic and Irish and speculated on the possibilities of putting a line-up together with that whole feel in mind. Our casual conversation seemed to forever drift towards the 'strange but true' variety and my rambling discourses, garnered from the paperback wisdom shelf, held a special fascination for her. From the beginning one had a sense that Sinéad was in the process of earnestly supplanting her own Catholicism. Sexually she was both innocent and knowing, and she was determined to use music to assert her individuality."

Sinéad in 1984, photographed by Irish psychic Zak Martin.

They spent the summer of 1984 recruiting members for their new band. Columb recruited Eamonn Galvin, an economics student and drummer, who ran a struggling rehearsal studio called Atlantis in Dublin's Crown Alley. His friend Kevin O'Byrne, an architecture student at Bolton Street College of Technology, played bongoes. Columb switched from guitar to bass and the band began to fall into shape. "The enthusiasm was ridiculous," Farrelly remembers. "Both the lads decided to quit college. We recorded a demo at STS with this primitive line-up. We didn't sound just raw. We sounded primeval."

Kevin O'Byrne had known Sinéad when she attended Sion Hill College. The last time he had met her was at the Top Hat roller disco in Dun Laoghaire, Co. Dublin. Sinéad asked Kevin to dance. She was a great skater, he remembers. They danced and talked. Four weeks later he met her at a party at a friend's house off Foxrock Avenue. After that they lost touch.

He was surprised when she turned up with Columb for that first rehearsal. "She was even more attractive than I remembered her – she'd learned how to dress and use make-up and she was far more feminine than she had been. At Sion Hill she had been a tomboy and her circle of friends were nearly all male. There was little of the tomboy now apart, possibly, from the Doc Marten's boots. She was intense, nervy and conveyed the impression of being keyed-up, on a hair-trigger." That hair-trigger could have exploded a live bomb or collapsed a house of cards, he thought, yet Sinéad had an air of vulnerability that made people feel protective towards her.

Sinéad and Kevin became close friends during those summer months of rehearsals, when they would often work into the early hours of the morning down in Atlantis Studios. Her only ambition, she told Kevin, was to become a rock star. "She talked to me about this a number of

Ton Ton Macoute in 1990; left to right: Eamonn Galvin, Kevin O'Byrne, Mary Downes and Mark Walsh.

times. She said it wasn't so much the money that attracted her to the idea of pop stardom, but the power to influence people and events that went with it." In his estimation her political views were naïve and simplistic.

Sinéad liked to dress in dark, sombre clothes and she rarely wore skirts or dresses. This had nothing to do with modesty or any reluctance to use her sexuality, according to O'Byrne. "She had a thing about her legs and her calves in particular, which she considered were too beefy and muscular – the result of years attending Mrs Smith's ballet classes."

Their rehearsals were often chaotic and subject to the whims of Sinéad. "Sometimes she would appear late at Atlantis, bounding in full of eagerness and discovering reverb or echo for the first time, and would invariably subject us to her favourite irreverent parody of a popular TV chocolate commercial ... 'Only the crunchiest, flakiest chocolate, tastes like lepers never tasted before' ..."

The band's line-up was augmented by Londoner Ashley Dweiss, a cittern-playing busker, and Breffni Murphy, a jazz enthusiast, illustrator of children's books and stained glass artist.

The band set out by calling itself 'One Hand Clap', from the Zen saying that 'It takes one ear to hear, one hand to clap', but this apparently produced too much tasteless ribbing from some of the heavy metal brethren who used the rehearsal space with them.

They settled on Ton Ton Macoute – a naïve choice under the circumstances but one based on "its strong and rhythmic sound", according to Farrelly. Others have different versions of the story.

Congas player Kevin O'Byrne remembers how the decision to adopt the name Ton Ton Macoute was taken almost on the spur of the moment, although it was among a shortlist of candidates. He remembers the band plumping for the name on the eve of their first ever live gig, a lunchtime session in a student canteen in Bolton Street College.

"We decided that Ton Ton Macoute was the more appropriate as it described a secret, magical organisation. We did not realise, at that stage, how much resistance there would be to this title with its negative links with the notorious 'Papa Doc' Duvalier regime in Haiti; we must have been naïve not to think of this but it simply did not occur to us at the time." Duvalier's regime had been built on a voodoo religion inspired by terror and augmented by his own private secret army, named after the shadowy zombies of that religion, the Ton Ton Macoute. Duvalier's men never removed their sun glasses, further fuelling local superstitions that they were captive souls in the power of Duvalier's evil rule.

Whether or not the rest of the band were naïve about the name, it is unlikely that Columb Farrelly was unaware of its connotations. The reverse was closer to the truth. Even if his only acquaintance with them was through Graham Greene's novel *The Comedians*, he was happy to choose a name that might arouse attention and controversy.

Sinéad returned, reluctantly, to Newtown that autumn but her mind was made up. She was going to be a singer.

"I didn't enjoy school," she said later, "because I was unhappy and had no interest in anything. All the time at school I felt I didn't belong there. I felt that I had a brain but in school I couldn't use it. The only things I was interested in were English and poetry and reading."

The band followed her to Waterford, renting a house in the nearby seaside town of Tramore called 'Ceol Tra' that boasted a large picture window with a panoramic view of the bay. The rhythm section of Kevin O'Byrne, Eamonn Galvin and Columb Farrelly rehearsed with Sinéad there, picking her up after school and hitching the distance to the house in Tramore every day. "The house," Farrelly recalls, "soon stank of roll ups and Eamonn's Doc Marten's."

When the band ran out of money and with offers of live gigs from Dublin, they decided to move back and Sinéad began to talk of taking off herself. She saw no point in continuing her stay at the college.

She began returning home at weekends, gigging and rehearsing with the band. Eventually she decided not to return, packed her bags and walked out, heading for Dublin.

Joe Falvey recalls discussing Sinéad with her parents in Dublin and chatting about the importance of getting her back to her studies to do her Leaving Certificate. He was told she would return that Sunday.

"I remember pacing up and down at the cold railway station waiting for her to come, and then at the other end of the platform I saw another pensive figure walking up and down and it was Craig Johnson, her boyfriend. I always thought that funny: here were the two of us waiting, me more the uncle figure, waiting with the boyfriend for this young one from Dublin and she didn't come." Sinéad did return in mid-week but her resolve to leave had strengthened.

Joe Falvey had a long talk with her in the staff dining room about her future. "The two of us sat here in this same room for two hours exchanging cigarettes. I was trying to point out in my schoolmasterly way the world that I knew best, that of education and the importance of doing the Leaving Certificate. It was something good to fall back on and if her musical interests didn't work out she would be glad that she had an entry requirement for college. I thought I was winning the argument but she said, 'No way, I'm not interested in doing my Leaving Cert, full stop.' She said, 'I'm a musician, I know I'm good, I want to make my livelihood at that and if I'm going to make my livelihood this is the time to do it. Things are beginning to happen for me and I want to give it everything and the time is now'."

Falvey, himself a minor impresario in his own student days, who has since revived his interest in music and promotion, warned Sinéad of the 'road to fame and stardom covered with the corpses of hopefuls and starry-eyed teenagers'. It was a difficult, tough business, he warned her, with a lot of sharks waiting to take advantage of gullible singers so that they could rip them off ... it wouldn't be easy to make it to the top.

Sinéad eyed him squarely, a waif-like 17-year-old and said, "I know that but the difference with me is that I'm going to make it. If the world is tough out there, I'm tough enough for it."

Falvey sat back in his chair, defeated. He knew she had the grit and determination and the dream, which, he says, he would love to have had at her age.

"I remember saying, 'Sinéad, if that is the way you are going, be sure to get a good lawyer.' 'Oh,' she said, 'don't worry, I have the best'."

"The difference with me is that I'm going to make it."

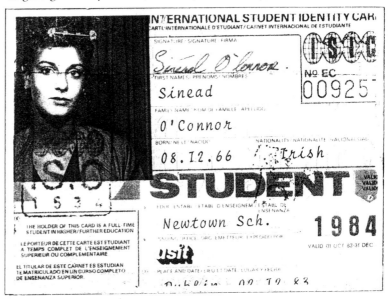

Chapter Eight

Just Like You
Said It Would Be

Ton Ton Macoute were paid around £100 for their first live show in the canteen of Dublin's Bolton Street College of Technology.

During the long summer in the Atlantis rehearsal rooms they had worked on Columb and Sinéad's material, explored various musical styles and, as Kevin O'Byrne recalls, "looked for an original sound, often not emerging until dawn." Sinéad's material, he remembers, "was quite rough and it was usual for Columb to take an hour or so alone with her to polish up her material before presenting it to the band." Farrelly, he recalls, was interested in the Arabic scale and Arabic chants and he spent some time teaching Sinéad how to sing in the style he had developed. By combining these with elements of Afro-Caribbean rhythms the distinctive sound of Ton Ton Macoute evolved and later still, he claims, the sound associated with Sinéad.

Before Sinéad left Waterford she called Columb and told him of her intentions. He persuaded his mother to put her up on the couch of his living room for a few days, a period his mother recalls to this day. Although Sinéad had been polite and well mannered, she lacked the social nuance for visiting a working class home in Dublin. For both parties it was a sharp cultural clash of social backgrounds – Sinéad, south Dublin and very middle class, Columb's family, northside and working class.

Columb next found Sinéad a bed in the home of his then girlfriend, Leslie Latimer, in Portmarnock. Leslie's sister, Clodagh Latimer, became Sinéad's closest friend for the next two years. She and Clodagh got themselves a small bedsit on Dublin's South Circular Road and later, when Sinéad moved to London, she and Clodagh shared a flat together for some time.

"We played our first gig on Friday, October 9, 1984," recalls Kevin O'Byrne. "It was only a lunchtime session at Bolton Street College but we were all very excited at the prospect of playing in front of an audience after all the work we had put into rehearsing."

About 80 students were present at their inauspicious début. "They were more occupied with munching on tomato sandwiches and sipping from flasks to notice that we had sweated blood to be there," Columb Farrelly remembers. Members of In Tua Nua had also turned up to lend moral support.

"Sinéad's hands shook as she offered me a cigarette," he says. "Every time she bought a new pack she would invert one of the cigarettes. She wore an off the shoulder, loose fitting dress in funeral black and the one or two apprentices who were awake enough to get a quick flash of tit during the third number almost choked on their sandwiches."

Although Farrelly remembers they were relieved to have got through

that début, and even how they backed over some expensive timber on their way out in their beat up old van, Kevin O'Byrne remembers … "discovering this powerful chemistry, a kind of magic between us as we performed on-stage which hadn't been apparent during rehearsals. We played our hearts out and the gig was a great success. It was a tremendous emotional release for all of us. Sinéad, in particular, became very emotional … I suppose because she had been vindicated in principle – she had proved to herself that she really could be a successful performer. She came around and hugged and kissed each one of us. This was to become a ritual after every gig."

Ton Ton Macoute poster drawn by Columb Farrelly.

Kevin O'Byrne claims that he and Sinéad became lovers about this time although this has since been denied by her, for reasons best known to herself, through a spokeswoman. O'Byrne recalls how they spent much of their spare time, day and night, together. "Usually I would stay overnight at her place to get away from the band. Her place was a dingy room on the South Circular Road. We had to share her kitchen and bathroom with another couple. Her room was always a complete mess, strewn with tapes of Bob Dylan, The Smiths and The Cure. She hated living there but it was the only alternative to school and her parents, so she made the most of it."

Sinéad was still experiencing pressure from her parents to 'straighten herself out' and 'get a proper education or at least a proper job' but she was determined to show them that she was independent and could make her own way in the world.

The band, meantime, spurred on by the euphoria of their début, continued to rehearse and work on their repertoire. Sinéad found herself a job as a waitress in The Bad Ass Café, a popular pizza parlour on Dublin's Crown Alley, an old cobble-stoned Dublin street in the shadow of the monstrous monolith of the Central Bank.

It was a convenient location, directly opposite the Atlantis rehearsal studio where the band spent most of their spare hours. They used to meet over coffees in the restaurant, huddled around a table plotting their scheme for world pop stardom and arguing the toss over musical directions. The owner was fond of joining these discussions and once offered them £100 to drop the name Ton Ton Macoute in exchange for his own choice of Soixante Neuf.

Ton Ton Macoute sang songs like 'VuDu 4U', 'Boa Constrictor' and 'We Are Afraid' drawn from Columb Farrelly's grab-bag of Celtic Goth mysticism and occult party tricks. He explained the snake motif to Sinéad, the sexual connotations of snakes, particularly in Egyptian and Celtic myths and magic. This, Kevin O'Byrne maintains, had a particular attraction for Sinéad who followed up Columb's occasional discourses by reading on the subject, particularly in the area of Celtic mythology. Sinéad was particularly chuffed to learn her own name, roughly translated from the Gaelic, meant 'white woman of magic'.

Farrelly has been hounded and haunted by his 'party tricks' since Sinéad O'Connor gave her first interview in 1986. One night in a Dublin hotel in November of 1989 he said, "Ever since it was first mentioned in an interview I haven't begun a single conversation with anyone without that subject being raised – I had an ordinary interest, I read some books, I had met some people on my travels who had claimed to be adepts.

"She was like a woman possessed; like those voodoo spiritualists in Haiti who are taken over by strange entities."

KEVIN O'BYRNE

"Beyond that there is no big deal, nothing. Some nights we would sit late, drinking coffee and we'd talk about things like that … the way people do …"

The band continued to gig. Sinéad's performances were marking her out for special mention. "They were energetic, to say the least," says Kevin O'Byrne. "She was like a woman possessed; like those voodoo spiritualists in Haiti who are taken over by strange entities. She often remarked that she felt as though she were two different people and the dominant one only came to the surface when she sang. She told me she was only ever really happy on-stage, performing … it was her therapy, her release mechanism."

Sinéad told reporter Barry Egan in 1988, "I change as soon as I get on-stage into a completely different person. I've no control over it, I just change. I just stand there with a black glare in my eyes … I don't know what it is. It's just that I think I could just get up and sing – scream! I get really nervous before I go on but when I go on 'she' comes along. 'She' thinks she's the queen or something. 'She' looks at me and she thinks she's very important. I know I'm a completely different person when I'm on-stage – I'm stronger, much more powerful. I'm tall, I'm beautiful, I'm strong … but it's all the same person, exactly the same person."

The next couple of gigs after Bolton Street were poorly attended apart from her friends in In Tua Nua, particularly fiddle player Steve Wickham and his girlfriend Babs, and piper Vinnie Kilduff who encouraged Sinéad and gave her confidence.

In Tua Nua, who by this time had been signed to Island Records, were persuaded to take some rehearsal space in Atlantis while they prepared to record demos for their début album.

Paul Byrne, In Tua Nua's drummer remembers catching some of those early gigs and hearing Ton Ton Macoute rehearse through the walls of the Atlantis rehearsal studios. "Columb was the main writer but he's a bass player and everyone had to build around the bass … they had an electric sitar and they had congas, so they were pretty unique. There was a lot of primal screaming coming through the walls, very punk and very experimental.

"It was very loud, raucous music but Sinéad was what held the whole thing down. I went to see a couple of their gigs, but then anybody that came to see the band just wanted her and that caused a lot of tension in the band."

Sinéad's father had by now become resigned to his daughter's musical ambitions. On the night of her 18th birthday in December 1984, in Tommy Dunne's Tavern, the band played a show watched by Sinéad's father and her stepmother. It was a particularly wild night, played, according to Kevin O'Byrne, "in a strange murky atmosphere." When a fight broke out in the pub, someone was stabbed. Sinéad introduced the band to her father and stepmother.

"He enjoyed the gig immensely," according to Columb Farrelly. "He seemed very proud of his daughter and reassured that she had not fallen into the hands of total yobbos … which was very generous of him as someone was being carried out with a knife wound as we spoke." Afterwards they all retired to the Atlantis studios where a birthday party was held. They drank freely and became drunk on home-made banana and fig wine. Sinéad, Steve Wickham and Kevin O'Byrne jammed for the guests and later Kevin gave Sinéad a necklace and a serpent bracelet she had asked for as a present.

The band were on a high, confident at the way things were progressing – they were building a following and getting more and more bookings. On December 19 they went to the recording studio at the National Institute for Higher Education (now City of Dublin University) to record a demo. Steve Wickham had been asked to produce it, but when it happened there were as many as nine people in the control room at any one time and the production and mixing duties were largely left to Sinéad and Columb.

"During the session the engineer was overcome with an acute attack of asthma, probably brought on by anxiety," says Columb who took off to the pub to await the final mix. Although the band were not entirely satisfied with the results on the tape, Steve Wickham was enthused enough to play it for U2's Bono the following day. Within weeks the rumours were flying – 'Bono to produce Ton Ton Macoute', 'Ton Ton Macoute are going to get a Mother deal'.

Their profile was rising and more people were turning up for their shows. There were candidates putting themselves forward as potential managers and agents for the band, including Kieran Owens, one of the best respected rock managers in Dublin.

A graduate of Trinity College and a former entertainments officer at the university, Kieran had been around the Irish music scene for some time and knew it inside out. During the late seventies and early eighties he steered avant garde performance artists and wild rockers The Virgin Prunes through their successful recording and gigging career, presenting a stark contrast of level headed sobriety against the band's image of anarchic mayhem.

Later, for a brief time, he handled the affairs of Cactus World News during their first years with MCA and later still he secured a lucrative album contract with China Records for Dublin dance duo Fountainhead. Today he manages another duo, Hinterland, signed to Island Records.

Owens saw Ton Ton Macoute for the first time at the final of a 'Battle Of The Bands' contest in Trinity's Junior Common Room, a large square room reached by a broad sweeping staircase above the arched entrance to the old university.

"I was strolling through the front arch of Trinity and I noticed a sandwich board for the band who were playing upstairs, as bands usually do there on Wednesdays at lunchtime," he recalls. As a former Ents Officer in TCD Kieran decided to have a look, out of curiosity and for old times sake.

His own band Fountainhead, a duo, had cut some discs already but had yet to play live. Their current single, 'Rhythm Method' was getting considerable airplay. Owens had the notion of checking out the band upstairs in the JCR at Trinity with the vague notion of seeking musicians to back Fountainhead.

"So I went upstairs and there were maybe 50 people sitting there – some were there 'cos that's where they sat at lunchtime in Trinity as always, and some were there to see the band. Within a song there was something chilling running up and down my spine and without any doubt the impact of the singer made itself immediately forceful on

Extracts from Sinéad's birthday cards to boyfriend Kevin O'Byrne.

me as a listener.

"She was extremely waifish, shortish cut hair, certainly nothing like the way she had it later … my overriding impression by the end of it was, how can such a powerfully staggering voice come out of the frame of somebody so fragile looking? She literally was just skin and bones, stunningly attractive, anyway … beside the fact that she was a very beautiful girl she had a very powerful voice," Owens remembers.

"I remember thinking of the previous time I was affected by seeing a girl singer. It was seven years earlier in London when I had gone to see a concert by The Tourists in London. It's my only claim to fame as a journalist because I wrote a review for *Hot Press* saying watch out for this singer because she's a steam train coming … the same sense of being in the presence of a really gifted singer."

Owens was singularly unimpressed by the rest of the band, though. "The rest of what was going on was not in any way impressive, it was competent but there was an extreme mismatch of visual styles. You had this very tense, beautiful and fragile girl with a guy who looked as if he was auditioning for the next *Doctor Who* … that's very unfair but it gives you some sense of the lack of awareness on the part of the band, of what they were and what their potential was."

Stunned and mesmerised, Owens went up to Sinéad after the show. "I said, 'You wouldn't know who I am …' it really was the ultimate cliché.I said, 'Hello, I'm Kieran Owens. I'm in the music business, I manage a band,' luckily not quite that crass but I did it in the nice diplomatic way that I hope is a feature of how I do things," he says, laughing."I told her 'I just want to say I think you are absolutely incredible and you've got an incredible voice and if there is any way that I can help … I don't know where you are playing again so I'm going to take the opportunity now to ask … can you let me know where the next set of gigs are …?"

Well, who could resist such beguiling patter? Sinéad reacted with embarrassment which, on reflection, was gracious of her. As Owens spluttered, Sinéad blushed."She was completely embarrassed … she sort of went, 'Wow, I appreciate the interest …' She was then as she is to me now – a completely self effacing, modest person."

Owens, a non-musician, prides himself on his ability to spot talent with a keener eye than an A&R man. His instinct told him he had found someone with *it* in bundles.

Ton Ton Macoute had a residency in those days at Dublin's Ivy Rooms, a small start-up venue where bands played before they progressed to the likes of the Baggot Inn in Dublin's Baggot Street. Kieran went along to see them a few times over the Christmas period.

Things were also beginning to happen to his own band, Fountainhead. Although still a duo with tape machines and keyboards and no live appearances, their single 'Rhythm Method' was garnering good airplay on Irish radio. Deals and offers were flowing in.

"I was introduced to Ossie Kilkenny around this time for dealings with Fountainhead. I knew Fachtna O'Ceallaigh very well from his journalist days and since The Rats thing. I met him at Christmas and he recommended two people for me to go and see. They were Ossie Kilkenny and John Kennedy, an English lawyer who has subsequently become the lawyer for many of the big bands who have come out of

Ireland, including Sinéad," recalls Owens.

With Owens' interest and his own growing list of contacts gathered with the increasing success of his own band, things were about to take another dramatic turn for Sinéad. Through his London lawyer, John Kennedy, Owens met Nigel Grainge and Chris Hill of Ensign Records. Ensign, and Grainge in particular, had a long history of contacts and dealings with Irish acts. At different stages Grainge, while at Polydor, had signed Thin Lizzy and later with his own label, Ensign, The Boomtown Rats, who in turn had been managed by Fachtna O'Ceallaigh.

Ossie Kilkenny was already Ireland's top entertainment accountant, representing everyone from Bob Geldof to U2. A former showband guitarist himself, although not for long, he soon swapped his guitar for a ledger. Kilkenny represented many rising young Irish acts in the seventies but his own star began shooting with the success, firstly of The Boomtown Rats and later, U2.

Sinéad O'Connor's success, while undoubtedly rooted in her own towering musical and singing talent, was fostered and nurtured and protected by the growing Irish 'Murphia' in the London music business. Grainge and Hill were among a group of record company executives scheduled to make the journey to Dublin in February for a special Fountainhead showcase at Dublin's Television Club, a large ballroom venue owned by former British TV star Eamonn Andrews and coincidentally beneath Eamonn Andrews' studio where the young Sinéad O'Connor had spent a happy summer with In Tua Nua.

Derek Green and Bob Grace of China Records attended the TV Club showcase too, and they eventually signed Fountainhead.

Grainge and Hill, however, wanted to pass on the band but asked Kieran Owens to recommend anybody else they should go and see while they were in Dublin.

"My reaction immediately was, 'There's only one artist that somebody should go and see, she is going to be signed and is going to be very successful because she just has it, she's got whatever it is you need. That girl is Sinéad O'Connor and she plays with this band called Ton Ton Macoute'," Owens says.

Sinéad and the band were playing their regular residency at The Ivy Rooms that night. Owens phoned her to say that some record company friends of his were coming to see the band and to see her. Up to this point Owens' only contact with the band on the few occasions he had seen them since that day in Trinity was with Sinéad. He more or less ignored the other musicians.

"I always identified her as the source of the talent because, to my ears, it was her voice that was the talent, not the rest of the band," he says.

Dublin rock promoter Kieran Owens.

"She was literally just skin and bone… stunningly attractive, with a very powerful voice."

KIERAN OWENS

Troy

The pace of change in Sinéad O'Connor's life, already hectic, was about to accelerate.

In the space of one year she had left school, joined a band and become a performer – she also held down jobs as a mini-skirted French maid with a kissogram company and as a waitress in a pizza restaurant during this time – and was now gaining attention from British record companies.

News that Bono had heard a demo tape of the band and was very taken by the music had reached them and this added to their kudos on the Irish scene. There was talk of Sinéad's father investing in the band.

Sinéad's own confidence was growing. She was prepared to challenge Columb more and more about arrangements and strategy and she was no longer prepared to be his mouthpiece – she wanted her own songs in the set. These confrontations could often be stormy, according to those who witnessed them.

Her belief in her own ability had increased enormously too. Paul Byrne of In Tua Nua remembers how she became increasingly outspoken whereas before she had been quiet and reserved. "She was getting this sort of edge, she was pushing you and pushing you and she'd question whether you were sexist, were you safe, were you crossing any lines and why weren't you ... she was always challenging and poking you, and the next thing she was doing it to the world ..."

Offers and expressions of interest came from more than just Ensign, according to other members of the group, but there is little evidence of this. They held a meeting at Eamon's house in Killiney to discuss their future strategy. Columb, Sinéad, Eamon and Kevin were present.

It was decided that a small delegation – Sinéad and Columb – would travel to London and do the rounds of the record companies with their demo and biog and try to drum up some concrete interest in Ton Ton Macoute. The rest of the band would follow later.

On the way back from the meeting they passed Sinéad's mother's house in Arnold Grove. Sinéad had not spoken to her mother for almost two years but she was now willing to make some reconciliatory gesture.

Sinéad crept up to the sitting room window and peeked in. Her mother and younger brother John were in the room watching TV. Sinéad crept away. "She was quite upset," remembers Kevin. "She felt like an outsider yet she could not bring herself to let them know that she was there."

Columb Farrelly was 'heartscalded' at the sight of her, on tiptoe reaching up to peer in at her own mother, who was sitting unaware watching TV and then tiptoeing back up the gravel path. Less than one month later Sinéad's mother died in a fatal motor accident, on Sunday

morning, February 10, 1985, on her way to Mass.

Sinéad had spent the previous night in her Sandymount flat with Kevin O'Byrne. She later recalled, "I was in a flat in Dublin where I was living. I was there with this boyfriend of mine and all of a sudden we started to talk for no reason about what we would do if our parents died. I got very upset for some reason, like really upset. We just had this discussion and the next morning I was going to see my dad. I was walking up to the home that Sunday and I just knew it and I was destroyed.

There's no way of saying this without sounding like I'm fucking kookey," she told Legs McNeil of *SPIN*. But it's true. I just felt like I knew the night before she died that she was going to die. I just knew."

Kevin returned home the following morning and received a phone call from Eamon who told him what had happened. The rest of the band attended a party that night in Portmarnock, unaware of events. Sinéad was expected to turn up. She phoned instead and Columb answered the call. He couldn't hear her properly for the noise in the room but he thought he heard her say, 'My mother's dead'." He told her he would ring her back. Everyone gathered in the hall as Columb made the call.

"When I got through," he recalls, "Sinéad sounded almost matter-of-fact in her shocked state. And then sort of angry. Her mum had crashed on the dual carriageway." Kevin phoned her father's house in Merton Road. She was very distraught but didn't want to stay the night at home and wanted to meet at a flat in Beechwood Avenue in nearby Ranelagh. "I don't know whether we got any sleep that night, she just cried and cried," he says.

On the Tuesday the band rehearsed, at Sinéad's insistence, for a show the following night. Her mother's funeral was held on the Wednesday afternoon.

The rehearsal did not go well. Sinéad was too upset to sing. All the band attended her mother's funeral and afterwards they all retired to Eamon's house in Killiney where Sinéad had a stiff drink before heading for town and a brief rehearsal before the show.

Several people remember that performance in Dun Laoghaire's Purty Loft as intensely emotional, spine chilling and stunning. "She began by introducing the band and then, quietly and indistinctly, 'This is dedicated to someone who I wish could see me now,' before launching into 'Boa' and her finest performance," says Columb Farrelly.

Above: Sinéad as a French maid kissogram girl and, below, as a waitress at the Bad Ass Cafe.

"Her banshee wailing would take over when she had forgotten a lyric and she'd turn to us with a shrug of apology. I shouted at her, 'Just go for it!' and she did. Anybody who might have dropped by casually not knowing what to expect will never have forgotten that gig, I'm sure," he says.

Kevin remembers the gig was full of emotion with Sinéad on-stage crying through many of the songs. Her father and brother Joe were in the audience and she sang 'VuDu 4U', her father's favourite.

All of In Tua Nua turned up for the show. Paul Byrne remembers that show as "… a very moving experience … She just battled through it, did the gig." The show had its lighter moments in the face of the general gloom of the event. Ashley Dweiss suffered from a weak bladder and during the show he began to get an irresistible urge to pee. Eventually he had to drop his cittern and head for the loo. He was talked through his journey there and back by Sinéad at the microphone, to everyone's delight. The set ended with the band's own rallying cry, 'Not Afraid'.

A few days later the band met in Sherries Restaurant in Dublin's Abbey Street. Sinéad brought along a suitcase full of things taken from her mother's personal effects and insisted on distributing them among the band. They were embarrassed but she insisted. She gave Kevin a bottle of Eau de Sauvage aftershave and Columb got a photograph of her as a seven-year-old, her face a mixture of impish mischief, fear and apprehension.

On the following Saturday, February 16, the band played that fateful Trinity 'Battle Of The Bands' gig, coming second to a punk band called Modus Vivendi. Sinéad dyed her hair a lurid orange colour for that show. Sinéad's days with Ton Ton Macoute were numbered from that day forth.

Their next show was at the Ivy Rooms and it proved to be their last. That night Sinéad was approached by someone from a London record company who wanted her to go to London to record some material, according to Kevin O'Byrne. Within a few days a showcase was organised for Ensign Records in Litton Lane Studios. Afterwards Sinéad, Columb and Kevin met with Nigel Grainge and Chris Hill in Sinéad's Ranelagh flat which she was now sharing with Clodagh Latimer.

Grainge talked about signing The Boomtown Rats and The Waterboys and Sinéad sat and listened in awe. He enquired about the lyrics of the songs the band sang and Sinéad disappeared into another room to get a pen and paper. She wrote down the lyrics to a number of songs in their repertoire including, Farrelly noted, three of her own.

Grainge passed on the band, giving them a 'suck it and see' attitude, 'perhaps in six months' time … more experience … different songs', kind of conversation. He was, however, quite taken with Sinéad. "She had thick black hair and she was so pretty – though she wasn't made up to look pretty. Then she sang. The songs were dreadful but her voice was incredible. It ranged from this kind of pure little folk voice to a banshee wail like something from the depths of somewhere. Yet she was so self conscious. If she could have crawled back into the corner and sang with her back to us, she would have."

Disappointed by the recent turn of events and disillusioned by increasingly bitter internal divisions within the band, Ton Ton Macoute slowly began to disintegrate. Since the death of her mother Sinéad had distanced herself from the band – becoming detached, spending more time on her own and writing again.

On February 23, two weeks after the death of her mother she, Eamon and Kevin went to see Joan Armatrading at Dublin's RDS. At the end of the concert the three of them stood at the back of the hall singing a Ton Ton Macoute song, 'Light Up My World'.

Sinéad was also looking around for advice about her career. Kieran Owens had attended a number of the band's concerts since that fateful lunchtime gig on January 17. She was also talking to Mark Clinton, In Tua Nua's manager, and of course, her old friends Babs and Steve Wickham. Kieran Owens had let her know that there would be interest in her from record companies and she might be well advised to consult people like Ossie Kilkenny and John Kennedy in the event.

Within the band, Ashley and Breffni Murphy had announced their decision to leave Ton Ton Macoute to form a jazz trio. It caused considerable strain. Columb, Eamon and Kevin wanted to get rid of Ashley and Breffni while Sinéad wanted to keep the band together.

Soon afterwards Ashley also approached Columb with the hypothetical suggestion that, if Sinéad were to sign a solo deal with Ensign, would they not be compensated in some way by the record company for the loss of their singer, or perhaps might they not all benefit as members of her backing band? "I was bewildered and angry," recalls Columb.

The band played a final gig with Sinéad at the Ivy Rooms. There was a bar extension and during the show Columb managed to bring the bass amp and speakers crashing down around his ears. It cracked them all up.

Things had changed irrevocably. Sinéad announced her departure and, although there were attempts at reconciliation, she had made up her mind to get out and leave the Dublin scene far behind her. Her mother's death provided the final push.

"When she died was when it began to happen. Things really began to happen," she told Legs McNeil. "Then I just knew that she was around. I could smell her. I knew she was sitting there. I just knew there was something in it and I almost felt her telling me to do something."

Since her mother's death she had been fired by a renewal of her religious faith. Shortly after her mother's death she gave Kevin O'Byrne a present of a religious medal, one of a pair which used to belong to her mother. One night in her flat Sinéad told him she had a bad feeling about the medals and she suggested they go down to the canal and throw them into the water, which they did.

For a while she worked on her songwriting in Dublin, using the facilities at the College of Music in Dublin's Westland Row, where she had been a student for a short while after leaving Waterford. One day she brought Kevin in and played him a new song she was working on. It was called 'Troy'.

Her father later referred to that song, included on 'The Lion And The Cobra' and released as her first single on Ensign, as being roughly autobiographical "… she loved her mother and her mother loved her but there was a turbulence and a passion in the relationship and in the family that sometimes hurt them both."

'Troy' is the quintessential Sinéad O'Connor song; wild and elemental, bare-faced honesty stripped to the bones, raw and savage, haunting and emotional: it is the Sinéad O'Connor song that most people remember because its primordial essence can evoke a thousand diverse emotions and frighten the living daylights out of those who listen to it.

With 'Troy' Sinéad said goodbye and good riddance to Dublin and Ireland. Before she left she contacted Kevin and Columb to tell them she was going. Kevin bought her a second hand Jewish medallion with the head of a cobra on it. Columb bought her a bracelet with a cobra motif. Ton Ton Macoute continued to gig, although they were soon to suffer at the hands of their former friend when she announced to anyone who would listen that the band had split up when she left.

"I don't know whether we got any sleep that night… she just cried and cried."

JOHN O'CONNOR

Ticket for Sinéad's last show with Ton Ton Macoute.

Never Get Old

Getting out of Dublin was probably the best thing Sinéad ever did for her career as a musician.

Since her first musical dabblings with In Tua Nua in the summer of 1983, the recording session in Fermoy with her teacher, Joe Falvey, the support slots in Waterford folk clubs and then the experience of more than eight months of rehearsing and gigging with Ton Ton Macoute, her confidence in herself and her own abilities had grown enormously.

Having to rely on herself emotionally for some considerable time through Grianan and the Waterford boarding school, Sinéad had also become a fiercely independent free spirit. This became a fundamental tenet in what she would often later refer to as 'her policies'.

In her efforts to resolve this independence with those people who had helped and influenced her throughout her brief career to date, Sinéad also built a convenient mechanism whereby she could rewrite her own history as it progressed.

Before she left for London this had borne no significance, but as she became better known and the volume of interviews and level of exposure increased, it became more obvious to some people and hurtful to others.

Her father has asserted, probably correctly, that no-one 'discovered' Sinéad, she discovered herself. Her good luck, he wrote, was that she was prepared for the opportunity when it came "having overcome family problems which would have swamped many a young girl."

Sinéad had resolved from quite an early age that she would become a singer and pursued that goal with single-minded zeal. She was helped by Jeannette Byrne and In Tua Nua. She was helped by Joe Falvey, her teacher in Newtown. She was helped by Columb Farrelly, Kieran Owens, John Kennedy, Pat Savage, Ossie Kilkenny, Nigel Grainge, Chris Hill and Fachtna O'Ceallaigh. She was also helped by U2 and particularly their guitarist The Edge.

Joe Falvey, her teacher at Waterford, had never delved into Sinéad's background, preferring to take people 'as they stand'. "I was generally aware that her early teens had been a difficult time for her because she had a rebellious spirit," he says. "She was an individual and she was adamant to assert that individuality in whatever context she found herself. I'm sure whatever difficulty she had prior to coming to Newtown stemmed from that personality."

For her father, the time she spent at Grianan and then Newtown, despite the pain and anguish it evoked, proved of value to her later. "She did go through a tremendous change pattern while she was at Waterford. That kid came out of that school and she never looked back as far as moral integrity is concerned. She's now absolutely and fiercely honest and she wasn't when she went into that school."

There is an interesting footnote to her stay at Newtown.During her time there Sinéad had a hand in reviving the student council, the school concert and the school's first graduation dance. Although she had left the school by then, she turned up that June in The Haven Hotel in Dunmore East, County Waterford, for the school graduation dance with her old boyfriend, Craig Johnson. Only two members of staff turned up, the headmaster and Joe Falvey.

"I remember arriving late that night and they had just finished their meal. Then I saw this girl coming out of the shadows wearing this lovely black dress, running up to me – one of my rare moments of embarrassment – and flinging her arms around me, 'cos we had been good friends and she had disappeared suddenly."

No-one has ever claimed to have discovered Sinéad O'Connor and indeed, no-one interviewed for this book made any such claim. Kieran Owens, who first put Nigel Grainge in touch with her and to whom Sinéad later gave a Gold Disc as a 'thank you', felt his part was 'fate' and his role was purely functionary. He heard and recognised an extraordinary talent and passed that information on to people who were seeking such talent. He had no doubt that Sinéad was destined for major success.

Paul Byrne remembers her upstairs in a Dublin pub venue. It is one of those stories that is so typical of people who chanced upon Ton Ton Macoute in 1984 or early 1985."They were coming towards the end of the gig, she had been staring at this guy in the audience and she suddenly turned to Columb and she was going 'play, play' and they started playing this amazing two-chord rhythmic piece where no-one was changing a lot. It was the best thing they had done all night because it was simple. She started singing and the lyrics were brilliant ... this incredible song just came out. I went up to her afterwards and I said 'That was the best song, what was the name of it?' and she said, 'I just made it up' and I said, 'What?' and she said there was some guy there she had a fascination with or was obsessed with in the audience and he had broken her heart. This guy was in the audience in front of her and she was having this thing with him ... there was just this vibe going on between them. She just made this song up on the spot and got the band to play along and it was the best song of the night.I had never seen that happen before, it was the second time she had dumbfounded me. She had 'it', even when she was 15."

The moral, if any moral was intended, is that Sinéad O'Connor *did* discover herself. She made herself up because there was no-one there to do it for her.

Leaving Ireland in the wake of her mother's tragic death had a cathartic effect on Sinéad. Her death, as she commented, marked a period of rapid and dramatic change in her career. Sinéad said she could sense and feel her mother around her, willing her to take action, to do something. It would be easy for armchair psychologists to strip Sinéad O'Connor bare of her persona and pretensions, to find out how the tragic fallout of alcoholism is visited upon its innocent victims – the children of alcoholics.

They become approval seekers, fearing authority figures, angry people and criticism. Confusing love and pity, they seek other victims to rescue, replacing their own sense of self esteem with an overdeveloped sense of responsibility towards others. They crave excitement.

They can compensate for many of these traits by appearing aggressive or irreverent in the face of authority; or mask their ability to express their feelings and emotions by ardent protestations of their ability and tendency to do so. Above all they fear abandonment, yet paradoxically seek it in their own disastrous relationships.

Such traits are not part of some psychologist's grab-bag of symptoms, however. They are the very real tragedies of thousands of people, everywhere. For every alcoholic there are at least four or five people in their lives who are directly affected by their disease and carry those effects into their own adult lives.

"My experience in growing up and everything else is that I was always in situations that involved violence of one kind or another, whether it was verbal or physical," Sinéad has said. "As a result of that I wasn't used to situations that didn't have that and I found it very difficult, so I was almost attracted to men that there would be an argument with. I almost thrived on there being some sort of, you know, problem."

Sinéad's background fits aspects of such child profiles as Jung's 'child-hero' who in adulthood is never wrong, rejects failure and has a strong urge to maintain control and manipulate, or 'the problem kid' whose

compulsive behaviour can lead to all sorts of personal troubles, such as an unplanned pregnancy. Then there's the 'lost child', alone and solitary as a child, aimless and indecisive as an adult.

Why, for instance, did Sinéad O'Connor shave her head? Was it the most astute image-mongering scam since The Beatles' identical haircuts or David Bowie's much trumpeted bisexuality? Or was it the depersonalising action of someone who had suffered transferred guilt, felt angry and inadequate and sought vindication in their public actions? Is Sinéad another victim, like concentration camp inmates (whom she resembles with her shaved head), insane people or Joan of Arc?

Sinéad has found some release from her own problems in her music. "I think I'm probably living proof of the danger of not expressing your feelings. For years I couldn't express how I felt," she told *Rolling Stone*. "I think that's how music helped me. I also think that's why it's the most powerful medium: because it expresses for other people feelings that they can't express but that need to be expressed. If you don't express those feelings – whether you're aggressive or loving or whatever – they will blow you up one day."

By addressing her own difficulties and finding out about herself by whatever means she chose to employ – yoga, meditation, Qabalah or numerology, spiritualism – Sinéad has found some measure of balance. The 'lost child' has the potential to become independent, talented and creative; the problem child can turn that boldness to the advantage of others by showing courage and taking risks; the hero-child can be organised and resourceful.

Her situation is not unique among rock and roll's tragic pantheon of heroes such as Elvis Presley, Janis Joplin, Jim Morrison, John Lennon or Madonna. All had difficult childhoods, were isolated, abandoned and some were abused. All followed a similar pattern of relentlessly pursuing a goal of public adulation that led, paradoxically, to their own isolation.

When Sinéad left Ireland to pursue her consuming goal of fame and stardom, she felt she was leaving at her dead mother's prompting but she was also putting the past behind her. She hadn't seen her mother much since she ran away from her in 1979 yet, "I had always gone back to see her and always felt a great love from the relationship," she told Legs McNeil in *SPIN* in April, 1990. "She wasn't a very happy person. She wasn't happy with her life. I always felt some understanding for her. I could never feel hatred or bitterness towards her. I just knew from a small age that she didn't know what she was doing and she didn't mean it. I always felt a great love and a great bond."

Sinéad had other reasons but most were intrinsically tied up with her mother's own tragedy. "I think now I can understand her," she told McNeil, "because I am a woman and I am a mother and the frustration that she must have gone through being in Ireland and the age, the generation that she was. There's no divorce and there's no abortion – no contraception – and now I can look and I can say, poor woman. What a shitty life she must have had. What a shitty life my father had. As a woman, as an Irish woman, I feel that she should have been able to go out with somebody else. She should have been able to remarry. If it was me, I would react in exactly the same way. Just bend the rules."

Arriving in London in April, 1985, at the behest of Ensign's Nigel Grainge, Sinéad was put to work with former Waterboy Karl Wallinger at Seaview, his old London flat, where he had an eight-track machine. Wallinger, a Welshman with a penchant for painstaking explorations of sixties music, was then working on The Waterboys' 'This Is The Sea' album. "She came up and she was a real ball of energy," he told *NME*'s Stuart Bailie, "and impetuous as hell. Then Steve Wickham came round, which is interesting, because that was how we (The Waterboys) met him. He was in town doing a gig with In Tua Nua and he came back and played the fiddle …"

Sinéad had written to Grainge six weeks after leaving Ton Ton Macoute: "Dear Nigel," she wrote, "I've left the band. I'm writing my own songs. You did say you would be interested in recording some demos of my stuff, so when I finish the songs will you do it?"

Following her own advice on the "need to be cheeky, even rude to get anywhere. You have to force yourself on people. If you want something, ask for it," Sinéad caught Grainge on the hop. Yes, he had said he would like to record some demos of her songs so, yes, he said, get on a plane and come over.

Steve Wickham, a quiet spoken Dubliner, who has known Sinéad since the very early days of the In Tua Nua summer, became a very close friend of hers in Dublin afterwards, especially during the time when tensions and arguments were rife in Ton Ton Macoute. He has subsequently made appearances on her two albums. Following that fateful meeting in Wallinger's flat he also joined The Waterboys. Sinéad also made contributions to Wallinger's 'Ship Of Fools' début for his new band, World Party, released in 1987 and subsequently sang on 'Goodbye Jumbo', the classic follow-up album, hailed by many as the album of 1990.

Grainge paid a visit to Sinéad that night at Wallinger's to hear how things were going. He was greeted at the door by a smiling Wallinger, who told him he was about to get a very pleasant surprise. Sinéad was in the middle of recording 'Troy', a song with an emotional vice grip that clasps your heart and chokes off your breathing. Grainge was captivated.

Two months after Kieran Owens had steered Nigel Grainge in the direction of Sinéad O'Connor, Grainge called to let him know they felt Sinéad was … "absolutely stunning, we're going to sign her to a publishing deal with Dizzy Heights (Ensign's music publishing company) and we're going to give her a year or two to write and develop and see what happens."

With Karl Wallinger of World Party in New York, 1990.

Chapter Eleven

Mandinka

Life cannot have been too easy for a young Irish girl living alone in London.

Initially Sinéad lived with an aunt before getting her own flat, a cold water dive in Stoke Newington.She befriended a cousin who was a Buddhist, who discussed his religious beliefs with her and she dabbled with tarot card reading. She was told she had a great future ahead of her. She was impressed.

She later told *SPIN* magazine that during this period of her life she met her ideal lover through her aunt. He was an older man, married with children and a church minister."He was the fulfilment of all my fantasies," Sinéad said, "because he was black." The affair lasted almost a year-and-a-half, she said, "and it was horrible and painful. I was madly in love, basically, and he wasn't." The affair ended when she realised he had no intention of leaving his wife, children, job or home. She turfed him out and he returned with a Hoover vacuum cleaner. She said she could never figure out why he brought the Hoover.

In those early days in London, Ensign Records were distributed by Island Records and press and publicity for Ensign artists was also handled by Island. Sinéad spent much of her time in and around the imposing white Victorian mansion in St. Peter's Square where Island had its offices, a few minutes' walk away from the River Thames between Hammersmith and Chiswick. Her future manager Fachtna O'Ceallaigh was also based at Island where he ran U2's Mother Records label.

According to one person who knew her in those days she was … "A nice person, a sweet little imp who had that 'this is what I have to do', self determining nature and was never overruled and who, even then, could manipulate people to do what she wanted them to do. She was a very determined person – she was like Madonna, her life was sacrificed at the altar of her career."

Sinéad had already become acquainted with U2's accountant, Ossie Kilkenny, who was likely to be a party to any negotiations conducted on her behalf with Ensign or Dizzy Heights.

Sinéad signed O'Ceallaigh as her manager in 1986.

Fachtna O'Ceallaigh was a former *Irish Press* journalist, who worked as a cub reporter on the *Evening Press*. He was one of the first Irish newspaper journalists to write seriously about the Irish rock scene, often to the frustration of his news editor who would have preferred his thin, long haired young reporter to get out and cover a few 'Corpo' meetings or the local District Court hearings.

He wrote a local music column – one of the first – and in the early seventies spent a brief period managing Donegal family folk band, Clannad. Around 1975 he was persuaded by a casual friend, Bob Geldof,

to go along and see his rhythm and blues band who were making a name for themselves around the city. They were called The Boomtown Rats and before long Geldof asked Fachtna to manage the band.

Fachtna had already done his stint managing Clannad and he'd also taken up the reins with top Irish traditionalists The Bothy Band for six months. With both of these acts he had felt out of his depth, too much in awe of their musical prowess.

With The Rats, more attitude than finesse, and with the gathering punk storm in London, Fachtna felt more at ease with his task. He and Geldof took off for London with a demo tape that had been recorded on a four-track machine.

After the two had exhausted their quota of Irish record business contacts – Dave Robinson at Stiff Records and Ted Carrol at Chiswick – the Murphia were thin on the ground in the London music scene at that time – they had a stroke of luck when they met Thin Lizzy manager Chris O'Donnell, who introduced them to Phonogram's head of A&R, Nigel Grainge. He was impressed and signed the band to his new Phonogram affiliated label, Ensign.

The Boomtown Rats went on to become one of the most successful of the new wave bands in terms of UK chart hits and sales. But this success didn't translate into vast riches, nor did it survive long into the eighties as the mantle of pop band and hitmakers assumed the role of millstone around their necks. In the anti-rockist, New Romantic phase and the early technopop phases of that decade, The Rats were … dinosaurs.

Fachtna began managing Bananarama. He knew Siobhan Fahey, an

Irish girl, and O'Ceallaigh found their style more suited to his own attitudes than those of The Rats with whom he had long since become disillusioned. This time he was able to bring a band managerial experience of the record business from the top level. "If they said they wanted to make a record with so and so or 'we want to write songs' … it wasn't any big mystery. I could help them make it happen," he said in *Hot Press*.

Fachtna was also helping them with their public image and, more importantly, negotiating their record contract for them. Once again he was steering the career of an act in whom he was investing considerably more than his professional time and experience: he was investing his emotions and his passion for the business too.

Then they dumped him. After managing them for a year and bringing them to the point where they were about to sign a deal which would start them off at £150,000, the three girls dropped him and he never received any commission. But what was worse was the sense of betrayal.

"It was the most hurtful thing that ever happened to me," he says. "It was more hurtful to me than any kind of break up of a love affair or anything like that because I felt so close to the three of them. I felt for once it was possible to work with people without any of the business crap attached to it or any of the suspicions attached to it."

The pain and hurt was enough for him to resign himself to never working in the music business again. After almost five years at the top of the music business he found himself dumped, down and penniless. It was a hard lesson.

Salvation, for want of another word in this case, came in the shape of U2 and their fledgling Mother Records, a label the band had set up with the admirable intention of giving young bands a leg up into the rock business. Fachtna joined Mother in October, 1985. While despising the music of U2, O'Ceallaigh liked the idea of the label and the prospect of earning money again after two years of 'surviving'.

Above: Fachtna O'Ceallaigh. Below: The Boomtown Rats.

Within two years, having overseen the release of singles by bands like Limerick's Tuesday Blue, Glasgow's The Painted Word, an avant garde outfit called Operating Theatre, The Subterraneans and the début single of Hothouse Flowers before they went on to sign to London Records, Fachtna was clearly dissatisfied with Mother.

In an outspoken and wide ranging interview with the *Hot Press Yearbook* that winter – in which he acknowledged he was "probably digging my own fucking grave" – O'Ceallaigh said he regarded U2's approach to the label as "too precious" and their involvement in its workings as "meddling". Fachtna went on to rail against the "Godalmighty attitude" towards U2 in Ireland which he found distressing, arguing that the old guard of showbands who had controlled the industry in the sixties and the seventies had been supplanted by some ill defined power axis involving U2, the national radio station RTE and *Hot Press* magazine. It was a theme he has never bothered to repeat – Sinéad O'Connor did, though.

Fachtna was promptly fired by U2 – "Fachtna fired himself" Larry Mullen told *NME*.

Heroine

Fachtna O'Ceallaigh's contribution to Sinéad O'Connor's career is immeasurable.

Apart from choosing an obscure song written by Prince for a little known and long forgotten Minneapolis band, The Family, as a cover song and first single release from her second album, 'I Do Not Want What I Haven't Got', O'Ceallaigh can almost claim some credit for that tear in the 'Nothing Compares 2U' video that melted millions of hearts around the world.

"Well, I was fairly fucked up," she told Q magazine. "I was under enormous stress, I'd just split up with my manager literally two days before we made the video. So my life was really falling apart. It was all quite apt. I felt pretty ghastly …"

O'Ceallaigh's style of management is very personal. He sees his duty as a manager is to nurture and protect the artist. He only came back into the music business because he felt he had a solid personal and trusting relationship with Sinéad O'Connor.

"I met and became friends with Sinéad O'Connor when she was just about to do a deal with Ensign," Fachtna told *Hot Press*, "and at various times she asked me would I be interested in managing her and I kept saying, 'I don't really want to get involved in all that business again' but eventually it seemed like a natural thing to do. We had established a really, really strong friendship as the basis for anything that would happen and that's why I was happy to do it.

"I feel," he adds, "a complete and implicit trust in her and she feels, I think, the same thing in me."

For Fachtna, management for an artist like Sinéad was crucial to her relationship with a record company. "When it comes to dealing with the record companies and all the day to day business – that's the last thing the lead singer needs to be doing. First of all because you don't have time and secondly, your record company can't possibly have the right attitude to you if you're going in all the time talking about money and all that sort of stuff."

Re-entering the music business again as a manager, he resolved … "To be more relaxed, even though I despise doing it, but I'll be more relaxed from the point of view of socialising with people from the music business. I'll be more aware of listening to what they say and then trying to find a way of utilising that person and their position … from a personal point of view I know that this time round there is no gypsy-like attraction about the rock 'n' roll lifestyle or any of that crap. I know I won't go through that again and I'm 100 per cent certain about that because it's not the way I think now."

But not everyone was happy with the prospect of dealing with

Chapter Twelve

Sinéad O'Connor \ Heroine

Fachtna O'Ceallaigh with Sinéad.

Fachtna O'Ceallaigh as Sinéad O'Connor's manager.

"I opposed the connection," Grainge told *Rolling Stone*. "I knew Fachtna from many years before when The Boomtown Rats were on Ensign. Fachtna gets very emotionally involved with his acts. He can be very inspiring but he can also be infuriating when he doesn't get his way." Grainge fought to have O'Ceallaigh excluded from any dealings with Sinéad or his record company. "I told Sinéad, 'I don't want to work with Fachtna and I don't want him to be your manager'."

"Fachtna is my manager," Sinéad told him.

O'Ceallaigh's first action was to negotiate Sinéad's recording deal. One minute she was in and out of Ensign's office and then she was gone and Fachtna was there. The following year Sinéad told Molly McAnailly Burke, "He's a very forceful kind of bloke – but not in a bossy way – he's really thrown himself into what I've been doing. He's insistent and knows what I need and what I don't. He gets things done and is helpful and encouraging. I'm pleased that I met him – if I hadn't found the right manager I think I might have gone astray a bit."

While Sinéad worked on her songwriting during her first year in London, Irish accountant Ossie Kilkenny is attributed with introducing her to Bono, lead singer with U2. Bono remembered the tape he had heard from Steve Wickham, the session recorded by Ton Ton Macoute in Dublin's NIHE nine months previously.

Bono rang Sinéad one day and invited her to sing on a track for U2 guitarist The Edge's first effort at composing a movie soundtrack.

"I met The Edge and his wife who are both wonderful people," Sinéad told *Melody Maker* in 1986, "and I discovered that The Edge is a fine musician in his own right." Sinéad did not reserve the same praise for the film, *Captive*, a European heiress kidnap psychothriller starring Oliver Reed. "The film was trash but the music for the film is excellent," she added.

"It's very keyboard based," she explained. "Edge worked very closely with this guy called Michael Brooke who's Brian Eno's right hand man. I co-wrote one of the songs and I think it's great."

'Heroine' was the name of the song she co-wrote with The Edge. It combines Sinéad's distinctive line in church confessional melody with that even more distinctive and Cathedral-like sound wash so favoured by U2, syncopated by The Edge's chopping guitar lines.

"I like 'Heroine' very much," Sinéad told Paul Russell in *Fresh* magazine. "Edge is nice and easy to work with. I was particularly pleased to see him do something in his own right instead of being just U2's carrier."

This later comment was an indication of a growing estrangement between her and U2, Ireland's major rock export, which had its roots in a variety of issues, not least her manager's growing troubles with the band and Mother Records.

"I co-wrote one of the songs and I think it's great," Sinéad repeated to Helen Fitzgerald of *Melody Maker*, "but again, though I'm grateful for the interest I don't want to be mothered under the U2 umbrella." *Hot Press*'s Bill Graham described 'Heroine', the film's theme tune, as "not so much a song as a piece of music whose attractions become more obvious with increased play." Released as a single, it made a small dent in the British charts although the movie didn't fare as well.

Sinéad's involvement with The Edge and the U2 machine – Larry Mullen plays drums on the 'Heroine' recording – later gave rise to false assertions that Sinéad's career had somehow been helped along by U2.

It was not an image the Irish supergroup necessarily wished to promote themselves. At that period and throughout the eighties, with the band's steady rise to the very top of the pile, any young Irish band found itself being tagged with a U2 label – either compared unfavourably or just plain compared as in 'U2-like soundscape'.

U2's domination of the Irish rock scene was so complete that whenever an Irish band or singer was interviewed they were inevitably asked, 'What about U2?' or 'Do you know U2?'

The unfortunate aspect of this sort of questioning was the temptation to exploit the unpolished and inexperienced interview skills of young musicians. As U2's star rose in America and everywhere else in the world, including Britain, the British music press felt as though they had been bypassed. Their role in the U2 rise was peripheral. U2's rise was a populist movement and as such usurped the ground the British music magazines long claimed as their turf.

So young bands like Aslan, and relatively experienced individuals like That Petrol Emotion, found themselves manoeuvred into expressing opinions about U2 based on information that was at best second hand. Then they were misinterpreted.

The truth was, as ever, somewhere in between the myth and the so called reality. U2's Mother Records was a potentially worthwhile and even altruistic conception, but it was never clearly thought out and even less clearly defined by the principal players. The early results were frustration and growing resentment as the promised deals appeared to go to friends of the band, although even they began to resent the interminable delays in getting product onto the street.

O'Ceallaigh stuck his neck out because he appeared to believe that what he was doing might be of ultimate benefit to the label and the ideal from which it sprang – it was a debate, he correctly asserted, that should be fought in public if only to show that mistakes could be made and rectified, and that those involved were human.

O'Ceallaigh wanted Mother to release singles by bands that were totally unlike U2. He wanted a label that was "young, snappy and obnoxious and causes people to stop and think" but he found U2's attitude "was geared to the kind of group they are themselves."

In frustration, members of U2 withdrew hurt from involvement with the label as the criticism mounted. Ironically, their own predilection for choosing, as O'Ceallaigh had warned, bands like themselves, reinforced the conviction abroad that anything coming out of Ireland sounded like and was patronised by U2.

As Sinéad herself put it, their success "… is a very great hindrance to music in Ireland. As soon as there's a band that has men in it they're either told that they're like U2 and that's bad – or that they're bad because they're not like U2." All the more reason then for Sinéad O'Connor to avoid any such labelling and even more so considering her resolutely independent pursuit of her career to that point. As her father later wrote in the *Sunday Tribune*, "If it really matters, the misunderstanding which journalists arrive at in thinking Sinéad was 'discovered' by U2 stems from that fact. However Sinéad was already signed to

"(U2's success)… is a very great hindrance to music in Ireland."

Ensign when Edge asked her to sing 'Heroine'." The importance in this assertion was not that her father was putting the record straight in any way but that he should bother to make this assertion at all. Important as it may have been for Sinéad to be considered her own woman and artist right from the start, her involvement with The Edge did help to raise her profile before the release of her own début album one year later. Her subsequent very public row with U2 in the pages of *NME* two years later didn't do her any harm either, as U2 were very quick to point out.

The row first arose from a comment by Sinéad to a reporter with *i-D*, a British style-maker magazine of the time, when she said she didn't like U2's music, describing it as bombastic. This drew criticism from people close to U2 and she found herself ostracised by the U2 organisation. (It might be useful here to note Fachtna's own view, as a manager of some experience, on the use of such magazines as a vehicle to publicise an act – identifying *The Face* and *i-D* as 'taste-makers' in the *Hot Press* interview, Fachtna said, "People in record companies read in *i-D* about some groovy group that played at some warehouse party somewhere and immediately their interest is heightened." The lesson has never been lost on Sinéad O'Connor.

At a U2 show at Wembley in 1987, Sinéad went backstage. "I went to talk to somebody and U2's accountant, Ossie Kilkenny, who was in a group of people shouted at me that I had no right to be there, considering the things I had said, abusive things about people who had helped me."

For such a resolutely independent person whose manager was involved in an escalating internal row with Mother Records, such criticism was not on. "Presumably they meant they had helped me by fucking honouring me with having done the song 'Heroine', and he screamed this at me in front of a whole load of people," she told Egan.

The row escalated to the delight of the British music press. The

U2. Left to right: The Edge, Bono, Adam Clayton, Larry Mullen Jnr.

October 29, 1988, edition of *NME* featured a determined and unsmiling O'Connor with the headline, "Fighting Talk: Sinéad O'Connor Vs U2." Just over the page they featured Part Two of a major U2 feature running from the previous week's issue of the magazine with a headline that read, "You don't actually believe Sinéad, do you? She's in the business of creating news for herself," a quote from The Edge while drummer Larry Mullen was, in his accustomed fashion, a little more blunt. He said, "I wouldn't believe anything that Sinéad says."

The Edge said he found the whole thing amusing and placed Sinéad in a tradition of press manipulators that started with punk and Johnny Rotten, who based their strategy on creating notoriety surrounding their interviews. By then Sinéad had said she had no respect for Bono whom she accused of "faking his sincerity".

Sinéad claimed that U2 were "not the way they seem at all", echoing Fachtna's description of the unquestioned 'air of correctness' around everything U2 did, when she claimed she was refused payment for her work on 'Heroine'.

"I can show you a letter from their solicitor," she told Barry Egan of *NME* in 1988. "When I did 'Heroine' with The Edge they refused to pay me any money for doing it! U2 listed eight reasons why they didn't think I should have any money," she claimed. "The seventh reason was that they saw the project as a fucking help to me! I said to The Edge, 'This is not happening' and he said he didn't even know it was going on!" The Edge also said he would personally organise Sinéad's payment, she said, adding that in the end he paid her more than she wanted because he felt it was a really shitty thing for them to do. "They have fingers in every pie – they fucking rule Dublin. There's not a band in Dublin who could get anywhere if they weren't in some way associated with U2," she added.

Bono was shocked and appalled by Sinéad's remarks. A close friend of his spent an evening in his Bray home and they discussed the gathering controversy. Bono expressed his horror at Sinéad's attacks, coming as they did from someone he admired and believed in as an artist.

Remarkably, almost two years before this whole row erupted Sinéad told Molly McAnailly Burke in that *Hot Press* interview in December 1986, "I hope someday to help out Dublin bands the way I was helped by Bono, Ossie and the like." The fall-out from the whole affair was a brace of legal writs finding their way across the Irish Sea and on to the desk of the editor of *NME*. They didn't come from U2 or Sinéad O'Connor, but Ireland's *Hot Press*. In two successive issues of *NME*, first Derry band That Petrol Emotion and then Sinéad O'Connor alleged that the Irish magazine was owned by U2 and that the band virtually dictated the paper's editorial stance.

The following month in the November 17, 1988, issue of *Hot Press* the magazine printed an editorial and an open letter to Sinéad O'Connor refuting her claims and raising other, wider issues which were central to the, by now, open conflict between Sinéad, U2 and whoever got caught in the crossfire.

Apart from there being no grounds for the allegation that *Hot Press* was owned by anyone other than its three named directors – Niall Stokes, Mairin Sheehy and Jackie Hayden – the open letter by *Hot Press* writer Bill Graham suggested that if she sought conspirators she should look closer to home.

Sinéad's publicist in Ireland was Terry O'Neill, another former Mother employee who had been shown a 'red card' by football loving Larry Mullen the previous summer. O'Neill was also representing Hothouse Flowers at that time and Graham, without naming names, hinted that there were shadowy moves afoot to furnish a Sinéad O'Connor interview for *Hot Press* if the magazine 'chose' to write a 'soft' piece on Hothouse Flowers.

Graham went on to suggest that Sinéad should not waste her time on facile conspiracy theories, pointing out that she herself had benefited from that same so called power axis of RTE, U2 and *Hot Press*, which she and her associates were quick to claim held a controlling and talent stifling sway over what was happening in Dublin's rock circles.

In the aftermath of this newsprint skirmish Sinéad contacted *Hot Press* editor Niall Stokes who later spoke to her at length on the whole subject. "I was completely convinced that Sinéad's stance on the whole U2 controversy was completely without contrivance," he wrote last year. "Rightly or not she was absolutely convinced that Fachtna had been wronged."

In his analysis of Sinéad's response he concluded, "To understand Sinéad O'Connor it is, I think, essential to recognise this fundamental quality – most people create defence mechanisms, veils behind which to hide their real feelings, screens to protect them from bitter reality … with Sinéad there are no defence mechanisms. Her instinct is not to hide or camouflage her responses, but to go on revealing more and more of herself no matter how painful or contradictory the end results might be."

She later made attempts to resolve the conflict. Last year she said, "I knew in the back of my mind that some of the things I was saying were not said for myself. I expressed anger with U2 because they had hurt Fachtna, who was a friend of mine. I was wrong to do that because, really, Fachtna should fight his own battles."

As if to echo these sentiments, Stokes suggested Sinéad had begun "to internalise more and more of Fachtna's abrasions and in the process developed an attitude of deepening suspicion and hostility to many people who would have seen themselves as her natural allies."

The manner was typically patronising of the *Hot Press* editor but it carried a strong element of truth. People who have been, and are, close to Sinéad O'Connor are well aware of her grasp of events and her almost obsessive need to control anything to do with her own career. For them the guileless and innocent Sinéad image doesn't wash. Fachtna O'Ceallaigh, with his wealth of experience in the pop business and the mechanics of image making, may have provided the ammunition but Sinéad's finger was on the trigger all the time.

Chapter Thirteen

Lion And The Cobra

"I remember the next time I met her in Nomis Studios in London and she had shaved her hair off and she looked at me and said, 'Why don't I give you a haircut, Paul?' and I said, 'no' and she said, 'You're just afraid'." – Paul Byrne, Texas Kellys.

"I went on holiday to Greece and I had my hair dyed black at the time. It was starting to grow out and I went to an Italian barber and asked him to remove the dyed bits. He didn't have a clue what I was saying and just shaved away. I loved it and I haven't looked back since. The record company loves it too – it gets a laugh." *Hot Press* interview, December 4, 1986.

"The reason I cut it sounds really boring but there was this geezer in London who I really fancied and who had the same hair style. So I thought if I cut my hair off I might have a chance. It didn't work but I liked the hair cut so much I kept it." *Fresh* magazine interview, November 1987.

"A while back when these people from a record company were telling me how to look more feminine, giving me all this advice. I just thought, 'Fuck you' and had it all shaved. It was good for me because it lets me play around with conventional ideas of masculinity and femininity. I'm much happier with androgyny." *Melody Maker*, November 1987.

"After O'Ceallaigh came on board, Sinéad finally defined her own look by the stunningly simple move of shaving her head. 'People always ask me if I shaved my head to look aggressive but I shaved my head because I didn't want another boring hairdo. I did it because I'd done everything else that I could possibly do to my hair. The way I looked didn't represent the kind of music I do. If you heard a song like 'Troy' you wouldn't imagine it was done by some bald woman but some other woman with long hair and the rest …" Q Magazine, March 1990.

"She was always playing with her hair. One minute she had a Mohican. That was only for a couple of weeks and then it all went – she walked in and she had shaved herself bald. We thought, 'Well, there's a statement'." *Rolling Stone*, June 14, 1990.

As many people would later point out, Sinéad O'Connor is a study in contrasts and contradictions – a gentle skinhead, child-mother, Bambi in bovver boots, a coarse tongued Madonna.

Sinéad began work on her début album in the autumn of 1986, firstly with Mick Glossop, a veteran rock producer (now 41) who numbered The Skids, The Ruts, Van Morrison and The Waterboys' groundbreaking 'This Is The Sea' among his production and engineering credits. His background was in studio engineering.

A meeting was arranged by Nigel Grainge between the two as soon as Glossop had been chosen to do the production. They met in a pub and Glossop's first impression was of a quiet young girl who seemed to be in awe of proceedings, but he also noticed that she came across as strong minded and opinionated.

Six months was spent on the production and mixing of the results before Grainge and Hill told Glossop that things were not going well. They weren't happy with the results and they were scrapping the whole project. Later he heard she would produce the entire album herself.

Since then Glossop has been branded "a fucking old hippy" by Sinéad who claimed he "had these very romanticised ideas of how an Irish woman singer should sound. It was all heavy arrangements and nice little Celtic melodies." That was in a 1988 interview in *Rolling Stone*. Two years later she told *Spin*, "He was into seventies music and people like Grace Slick and Joan Baez and he thought I should make a record like that, a kind of Grace Slick sort of album."

Grainge and Hill at Ensign were no less scathing in their criticism. "The tracks sounded like a cabaret rock version of these wonderful songs," Grainge told *Rolling Stone* last year, while Hill added, "She was a young girl of 19 years who was pregnant and frightened that if she fucked up she was gonna lose her record deal and be told to go back to Ireland."

Sinéad had become pregnant by John Reynolds, a former drummer with Transvision Vamp, shortly after he joined her studio band. "It's a worrying thing for a man to have some girl come up and say, 'I'm having your baby'," Sinéad told Legs McNeil of *SPIN*, "but I remember taking him to this dingy, depressing café where we drank some horrible greasy tea and I was crying and said, 'I'm pregnant.' I was terrified. I mean, I was glad. I was really glad I was pregnant but I knew that I'd get a lot of trouble about it. I knew that there'd be trouble."

Happy as she was, it was a tremendous shock. Only six months earlier she had said that a good time to start a family would be when she reached her mid-twenties. "I want children myself," she said, "but right now I have to think of my career." But she was nonetheless very happy to have an unexpected pregnancy – in the past she has alluded to unspecified "gynaecological problems" and a pregnancy at this stage of her life may have prompted a resolution of those problems.

However, John Reynolds can hardly have been delighted with the situation he found himself in. "I could understand John's reluctance," Sinéad said. "Suddenly his whole life was flashing before him." As it turned out Reynolds stuck by her and was of invaluable help to Glossop during the recording of that 'difficult first album'.

Grainge and Hill hit the roof. "I was the only one that felt completely sure and delighted about the idea of having a baby," she said. The record company, their licensing deal with Island Records drawing to an end and with thousands already spent on demoing and the initial recording of the début, put severe pressure on her, with the help of the Ensign Records company doctor, to terminate the pregnancy with an abortion.

Sinéad told American TV host Arsenio Hall, "When I became pregnant I went to the record company doctor and I said that I was pregnant and that I was very happy about it. I was 19 at the time and I had just started recording my first album. I went to the doctor and he said that he was very happy that I was pregnant. Then when I left he phoned the record company and told them that I was pregnant, and they said to him to talk to me and try and talk me out of having it.

"The next time I went back to the doctor," she continued, "he said to me that I shouldn't have the baby, in fact that I couldn't have my baby because my record company had spent £120,000 on my album and I owed it to them not to have it. At the same time another man on the same label, his girlfriend was having a baby, and nobody said to him, 'You can't have your baby, we've spent £120,000 on your album.' I don't fucking get it. It's up to me to decide whether or not to have a baby – nobody has the right to make that decision for me, because of money.

"They said they'd invested all this money in me and that I was being very selfish to want to have a baby." Sinéad also claimed that she was told "a lot of shit about how I would die if I went on a plane."

Sinéad was deeply upset. Once more the troubled Irish waif had landed herself in it big time, and once more she survived by the strength of her own resolve and phenomenal will power. "I was very upset and hurt," she said later. "How could I choose between my career or a child? They're both as important as each other. It wasn't a Catholicism thing – I had nothing against abortion. In fact I was actually in the hospital bed about to have an abortion and then I left. It wasn't me that wanted to have it. I wanted the baby – and I decided to have it."

By her own admission, her moods and physical condition made the recording of the début album very difficult. Following the often bitter rows to keep her baby, Sinéad was less inclined to communicate her dissatisfaction with the progress of the recordings.

Glossop remains bemused by the whole episode. He groaned resignedly when descriptions of his production work on the album – ranging from 'utter shit' to 'Celtic rock' – were read to him.

Grainge and Hill approached him halfway through the mixing stage of the album. "We had quite a professional chat," he recalls, "and initially they were concerned that it was a question of how it was being mixed. And I thought they were unhappy with the performance or the arrangement sense but it seemed to be a lot more complicated than that ... we had a go at remixing some of it with a different engineer (Graham Dickson) ... it was all a bit weird.

"She wasn't all that difficult but slightly strange ... I felt she wasn't involved enough at times. She'd be upstairs playing pool with the rest of the band and sometimes I had to go along and say, 'Look, this is your album' but she'd say, 'Don't worry, don't worry, if I'm not happy, I'll tell you.' I think she was afraid to say anything at the time," adds Glossop.

An accurate assessment in retrospect. Sinéad later said about those sessions, "I didn't want the album to sound the way it sounded but I didn't say anything for weeks because I thought, 'Well, if the record company is happy with it they know more about this than I do, so I shouldn't say anything,' then they said they didn't like it. It was just shit,

Sinéad's husband John Reynolds with their son Jake.

"(The record company)... said they'd invested all this money in me and it was very selfish to want to have a baby."

it was all fucking Irish, ethereal and mystical."

It had never occurred to her that she had the right to question. She deferred to Glossop, she said, because "I was stupid. I was ignorant and they played on my ignorance." While Glossop regrets the "waste of time" he feels sure that some good came out of it. "Sinéad found out that that was not the way to make a record for her. I think that at some stage of her career she had to go through that, she had to realise that working with a producer under those sort of terms wasn't the way to do it … I see myself as being miscast, if you like. They should have let her just go and do it, it would have saved a lot of hassles but it was an interesting experience."

One thing that has rankled him since that episode are references to the production on certain tracks which suggest he had a stereotyped view of what a female Irish singer should sound like, that is, all fiddles and reverb. "Now the fiddles, there were two people who played fiddle on the tracks that we did, one called Bobby Valentino who I brought in because he's a very good player. The reason I brought him in was to provide a contrast to Steve Wickham of The Waterboys. Steve is an inspired soloist kind of violin player but he's not very good when you want him to play specific parts because he wanders about, he's not disciplined enough to stick to the part," he explained.

"The reason we brought Bobby in was, Sinéad had done a demo of 'Mandinka' and it had some parts on there which she wanted to be violin, so we brought Bobby in to do those parts. They did an extended end to the song which we were to use as a 12-inch mix and I said to Bobby, 'Play some solo bits over that,' and we did two or three tracks and it sounded brilliant. I remember Sinéad saying that sounds brilliant … it sounded like some movie at the time … they were the fiddles we put on. Steve was on the album because she wanted him on it, so for her to say I was the person who brought the fiddle player in because I had this stereotype idea that there should be loads of Irish fiddles on it I thought was very unfair, a) because she was very happy about it and b) because it was her idea in the first place."

He also carries reservations about the charges of 'cabaret rock' stating that such things are a "matter of taste". "If you put the two together and compare them, then there is a way in which you can say that comparison could be made," he concedes but argues that the album he put together was a rock album because when he met Sinéad she was rehearsing with a rock band and his album was a band album, unlike Sinéad's which he describes as a solo artist's album.

"It sounds like a solo album … you could argue that that's the way I should have approached it, but she was working with a band and all her songs were worked out in a rock format and that is the way I approached the album."

Although Glossop is reluctant to spell it out, he feels the role he was miscast to play was that of 'villain'. When I told him of the pressure Sinéad had come under regarding her pregnancy and the financial commitment of the record company to her career, he said, "So they admit that then?"

He agrees that it was the influence and persuasive powers of Fachtna O'Ceallaigh that prompted Grainge to agree to allow Sinéad to produce the album herself.

In retrospect he says, "Obviously the way she did it was the way it should have been done. She is, and she is going to be, more of a unique artist who can only be unique by doing it her own way. She's the sort of person who's always got to do things her own way. She has got something to say and she should be around for years."

On the recording sessions themselves, Glossop says, "I found the vocals difficult. It is very easy for her to sing extremely well but she has to have an audience. I remember when we were rehearsing one day a couple of press people from Chrysalis came down. It was about the time people realised what she was about and that this artist was going to do something ... she just played them a couple of songs with the band and they were amazing performances – that is all it takes with her."

In the studio, however, things did not run as smoothly. Sinéad has claimed there were "huge, huge arguments". Glossop remembers "difficulties" but not in any "stroppy or rude sense". "In the studio it was hard work, it was like 'the echo's wrong on my voice' and 'I can't hear the track enough' like 'I can't do it unless it is right'. I know there are a lot of artists like that who are lesser singers and they have to go through all that to boost their own confidence, to be able to perform ... she didn't."

Sinéad's band also underwent some line-up changes between the Glossop sessions and her own production of the album. She had begun with John Reynolds on drums, Ali McMordie (ex Stiff Little Fingers), and Marti Williamson, a session man who had worked with Psychedelic Furs and Steve Wickham (then with The Waterboys). The line-up on the album was Mike Clowes on keyboards, John Reynolds on drums, Rob Dean on electric and acoustic guitars, 'Spike' Hollifield on bass with top session man Marco Pirroni lending a hand on 'Mandinka', Kevin Mooney on 'Just Call Me Joe' and Irish singer Enya speaking on 'Never Get Old'.

In April 1987, seven months pregnant, 20 years of age and with more studio experience and savvy than people were willing to give her credit for, Sinéad began the production of her own album.

The Lion And

The Cobra (Again)

The birth of Sinéad's début album, 'The Lion And The Cobra' almost coincided with the birth of her son, Jake, on July 18, 1987.

After the Glossop debacle the pressure was on to deliver an album fast. Despite the loss of four months' recording and mixing, the decision was taken to let Sinéad do her own production.

Before this decision was made, recording engineer and producer Graham Dickson (Elton John, The Waterboys, Joan Armatrading) was called in to remix some of the Glossop tapes. He did two tracks.

There was one in particular that he recalls: 'Sex Jam' which became 'I Want Your Hands On Me' in the record's final cut. "I just remixed the masters after Nigel played the original demos for me," Dickson recalls. "It was clear there was a big difference between the tapes and the later production. There was something very special on the demos. I tried to put that unique sound back into the remix." Sinéad, he was told, wasn't happy with the treatment of the vocals on the Glossop recordings and the overall sound. Dickson's remix was instrumental in persuading Grainge and Hill to go ahead with the project. Sinéad thus came within a whisker of having her recording career shelved.

It was Fachtna O'Ceallaigh's powers of persuasion, Dickson's remixes and Grainge's own gut instinct about the demos, that prompted Grainge to tell Sinéad to get a good engineer and produce the album herself.

It was a major risk for Grainge to allow an unknown artist, 20-years-old and seven months pregnant, loose in a studio, but it's a measure of his confidence in Sinéad's ability that he did so. "I give Nigel more credit than I give anyone," concedes Mick Glossop now. "Nigel is always looking for different artists and he has got a lot of imagination, he is prepared to sign people that other people won't sign and he is prepared to take something on for that."

Sinéad had more studio experience than anyone appeared to give her credit for. Since the early days in 1983 in Eamonn Andrews' studios in Dublin with In Tua Nua, she had soaked up information and developed her control room savvy. Later, during the winter of 1983, she had demonstrated her new found studio skills in Brian O'Reilly's Fiona Studios in Fermoy when she had piloted her own demo, to the amazement of her Newtown schoolteacher, Joe Falvey.

'The Lion And The Cobra' was an outstanding début, thoroughly original. It swooped in out of left field, primitive, raw and searing. Sinéad's vocal style drew comparisons with the ethereal liltings of Liz Frazer from The Cocteau Twins and the other-worldly operatic wailings of Kate Bush. The songs were as hard as anything The Clash could deliver in their finest hour and as revealing as Dylan. The music and the sound of Sinéad O'Connor was unplaceable – amid Celtic swirls lurked strings and lush orchestral passages, hip hop drum beats, grungy guitar licks and often strongly eloquent silences. Elements and emotions beat around her head and by turns roared, wailed, squealed and whimpered from headphones and speakers everywhere.

Reviewing the album for the *Irish Press* on October 21, 1987, I described the album as ... "A staggering début, honest and warm and intense in its lyrical sentiment ... her voice by times shrieks, swoops and whoops its way through a host of curious tales of abandonment, betrayal, sensuous desire and curious bewilderment ... it will leave you breathless and just a little intoxicated."

As Sinéad had left Dublin before becoming a recognised figure on the Irish music scene, her début was greeted with interest but no-one was lighting bonfires. Earlier that year I had met Sinéad O'Connor for the first time at a Pogues' concert at Brixton Academy on St.Patrick's night, March 17. She was a few months pregnant at that stage, quiet, timid and enchanting. It was a wet, cold night and every tribe and sub-cult of London night life was out to see The Pogues on this night of all nights. Inside, the crowd was a seething mass of wild, jigging dancers and mayhem makers, and many had tried a drink or three in the manner of chief Pogue Shane MacGowan. Myself and Fachtna O'Ceallaigh, unable to converse amid the din and clamour, formed a protective cordon around the pregnant Sinéad and made our way to the back of the sloped hall to the bar. We stood there against the rail at the back for the duration of the show. Sinéad spoke quietly about pregnancy and her own apprehensions. I was full of the joys of fatherhood, having attended the birth of my first daughter only one month before in Dublin. I tried to reassure her.

Hot Press greeted her new release with a lukewarm review from Cathy Dillon. She described the album as "self consciously arty" while suggesting that its intensity and raw-edged intelligence "was just the anti-dote for all the Stock, Aitken and Waterman music (then) clogging the airwaves and the charts." Dillon found the album's overall melancholy air a bit hard to take and while she found the mixture of old and new, Irish and biblical "truly exotic", she believed it took itself too seriously for its own good. "'The Lion And The Cobra'," she concluded, "is solid evidence of Sinéad O'Connor's emerging talent."

Other writers were less restrained. Pam Lambert in *Rolling Stone* described the début album as "startling" with "light, Pretenders-style pop on 'Mandinka', syncopated dance funk on 'I Want Your Hands On Me' and symphonic strings on the six-and-a-half-minute long 'Troy'.

"O'Connor," she wrote, "twists conventional song structure and stretches pop singing while maintaining her melodic sense: on 'Just Call Me Joe' her voice is a lullaby croon; on 'Never Get Old' it soars above the jazzy piano chords into ecstatic, wordless cries."

Lambert was also quick to spot the faint Irish aura in some of the music, most notably in 'Never Get Old' which featured the voice of Enya speaking the words of Psalm 21 – the psalm quoted on the sleeve of the album – in Gaelic.

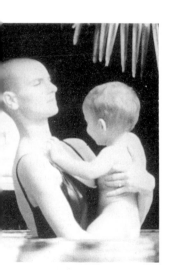

'... *for He will command His angels*
concerning you
to guard you in all your ways;

they will lift you up in their hands,
so that you will not strike your foot
against a stone.
you will tread upon the lion and the cobra;
you will trample the great lion and the serpent.'

The psalm is a prayer in the face of adversity and struggle and confrontation. Sinéad O'Connor knew and almost invited these things to thrive creatively.

Sinéad dedicated the album to her mother. On the sleeve notes there was a "special thanks" to John Reynolds and their baby, Jake, but an "extra special thanks" went to "Fachtna, my greatest source of encouragement and criticism, my biggest influence and my best friend."

The album was 'born' two weeks before Sinéad gave birth to her son, Jake, and the production, once she took control herself, was far less painful than the birth of Jake.

"It was frightening," she told Liam Fay of *Hot Press*. "I really thought I was going to die. And the worst thing is that they don't really tell you that it's going to be bad. I was told that childbirth is like a sexual experience – I don't know what kind of sexual experience these people have but I've never had anything like it. Take it from me, having a baby is fucking agony." Sinéad felt her body was in shock for a whole year afterwards.

It is arguable that Sinéad, the child adult, was having physical difficulties growing up that reflected her own psychological difficulties about moving from adolescence into adulthood. It wasn't the first time she had alluded to, without elaborating on, gynaecological difficulties that she had experienced prior to and after the birth of Jake. While she has been far more open and frank about her own bodily functions in interviews than most artists would dare, she is also deeply protective of her physical privacy. Bearing the brunt of a tirade from her in a Dublin pub one night last year, she repeatedly stated that just because she's famous doesn't mean people have a right to know what's going on in her womb.

Which is fine and accepted until you come to consider a song like 'Three Babies' on her second album, 'I Do Not Want What I Haven't Got' in which she speaks of 'Each of these, my three babies I will carry with me for myself, I ask no-one else to be mother to these three' and later, 'In my soul, my blood and bones, I have wrapped your cold bodies around me ...' It is a chilling and sorrowful tale and the song was, significantly, ignored by reviewers when the album was released last year.

Sinéad herself refused to explain the song in any detail to 2FM DJ Dave Fanning, saying it was not her policy to explain her songs in such detail while adding that it would also be embarrassing. To *NME*, her reference to the song was even more cryptic, "'Three Babies' sounds like a painful song but it's just thinking about emotional things that happen to you from a spiritual point of view. Seeing that there was a good thing in it. That it was a good thing that something shitty happened because you learned from it and it drew you towards something that you might not have been drawn towards before."

However, she later acknowledged on the ITV weekly arts programme *The South Bank Show* that her writings are drawn from personal

"Take it from me...
having a baby is
fucking agony."

Sinéad performing at
Dublin's Olympic
Ballroom, February
1988.

experience and that 'Three Babies' which, "everybody says is a very sad song but to me it isn't. It's just a song about a very awful experience, or series of awful experiences, which I needed to work out for myself … it's almost a form of self learning, of learning how I operate."

Fachtna O'Ceallaigh was supportive throughout the pregnancy and the production of the album but it was clearly an unpleasant experience for Sinéad. She has said she almost made it to the operating table for an abortion before she relented and made the decision to have her child, despite the pressure from her record company.

'I will stick by my own policies,' she sang later in a scourging rant against the music business: '… millions of people to offer advice and say how I should be, but they're twisted and they'll never be any influence on me …' and '… through their own words, they will be exposed, they've got a severe case of the Emperor's new clothes.'

The recording of 'The Lion And The Cobra' never ran smoothly. "I had problems communicating with the musicians which caused the split up of the band," she told *Hot Press*'s Bill Graham. "Until I had decided to produce the album, I had very much left them to their own devices … then it struck me it was my record with my head on the block. A lot of them couldn't handle that. They were quite patronising in that they thought they had more experience and I just shut up."

But apart from knowing what she didn't like about Mick Glossop's recordings, she later confessed, "I didn't have a clue about what sort of record I wanted to make. I wanted to make a simple record and I didn't want to make a seventies record or a typical Irish woman singer's record … I didn't want a record with loads of melodies, overdubs and four or five vocal tracks. I wanted it to be simple so that songs stood out … the songs are very emotional and they would sound as good with a guitar and vocals as with a big production."

Pregnancy, and the prospect of kicking against the pressure from her record company and those who would have had her packed away on the next boat back to Ireland, made Sinéad feel strong and strengthened her resolve to finish what she had started, to make her record her way.

Recalling that period she said, "Being pregnant made me feel strong, because having a baby is such a big deal – it's like the biggest thing that ever has or will happen to me. It makes everything else seem trivial. After fighting to keep the baby and going through the pregnancy and labour I felt like, hell, I can do anything I want."

Recording the album was physically exhausting and a mental strain. Sinéad was moody, exhausted and anaemic and the strain told in the relations between herself and the band – when she shouted instructions it was patronisingly passed off as the humours of pregnancy.

Over two years later and looking back to the recording of that auspicious début she recalls not having given it her full and undivided attention. "I just sat around reading pregnancy books most of the time. Physically, the album always seemed remote to me even while I was making it."

This was not surprising in some respects since many of the songs were written when she was 15 or 16 and capture all the tortuous adolescent angst and naïve, overblown imagery, the painful experiences of her past. It was an exorcism of her past, a psychotherapeutic expulsion of childhood pain. Sinéad has, by turns, acknowledged and denied as much.

Above: on stage at London's Dominion Theatre, 1988 and at The Sadler's Wells Theatre.

"It's impossible not to bring my past into my songs but it's not a time of life that I want to celebrate as a creative source. It was a fucking awful time," she told *Melody Maker*'s Paul Mathur.

'The Lion And The Cobra' was an astonishing record, a bizarre mish-mash of styles and genres, from folk to hip hop and grungy rock dirges. In the nature of the primitivists in the art world, 'The Lion And The Cobra' set out, unselfconsciously, to reinvent the concept of pop music without rules or structure. At times, as in 'Just Like U Said It Would B', 'Jerusalem' or the sublime 'Troy', it worked with devastating effectiveness.

Other tracks managed to retrace the steps she had worked to avoid, such as the distinctly Celtic 'Never Grow Old' or 'Drink Before The War' while 'Jackie' – about a drowning fisherman? – though disguised behind a grungy guitar, is unmistakably written in the Gaelic ballad style. 'Never Grow Old', which employs the multi-layered vocals of Enya Ni Bhraonain, is awash with those symphonic strings and Sinéad's own voice soaring and wailing in an Arabic style that could easily be traced back to her work with Ton Ton Macoute.

There were omissions from the final mix such as 'Sit Easy Beside Me', a song with a strong religious flavour based as it was on the line 'I made a promise to my servant that I would not let him die' from the Bible. Another interesting track recorded for the album was a version of the Irish ballad, 'She Moved Through The Fair', since popularised by Van Morrison and recorded by Sinéad with her sister Eimear accompanying her on harp.

Shaven-headed teenage mother in Dr Marten's boots, Sinéad O'Connor did not fit the headline-grabbing profile of that year's crop of precocious teen popettes like Tiffany, Debbie Gibson, Elisa Fiorello or Kylie Minogue, nor did songs like 'Troy', the first single release from the album, sit easily amid the disposable formula dance music which made up most of the British singles charts.

Sinéad was in direct contrast to all of this, not only visually but also insofar as her songs were too disturbing and real for the teenybop market, too grown up and adult. Those within her record company with some degree of aesthetic taste knew they had an Artist on their hands, and an Artist with a capital A. Marketing people, to whom the charts were a major preoccupation, would have shrugged and accepted the album as the folly of those in the higher echelons.

But 'The Lion And The Cobra' was a rare bird that demanded attention and got it. Expecting modest album sales and single releases as promotional vehicles, the record was swamped with ecstatic reviews and hailed as a *tour de force* for a début. The single 'Troy', all six-and-a-half-minutes of it, did little but the follow-up, 'Mandinka' swept Sinéad into unfamiliar territory once again – number 17 in the British charts.

As a vehicle for her vocal talents and a herald of a new talent demanding to be noticed, 'Mandinka' was perfect. This curious looking elf-waif with the beatific face, bald head and incongruous footwear was also an added curio for the *Top Of The Pops* freak parade. And better still, no-one knew what the song was about – it just sounded good.

The wise and knowing knew, or at least pretended to, while the curious pop seekers went out and bought the album. They found therein an awkward cuckoo for their record nest that sat uncomfortably with their Kylie discs. The cognoscenti rock fans, hip enough to pick up on the album, were also delighted, if initially confused. 'The Lion And The Cobra' with its emotional explorations of love, lust, anger and yearning was no instantly accessible piece of pop fluff. You had to work for your money.

The inevitable comparisons with Kate Bush and Liz Fraser were drawn but it was the album's unlearned, awkward and edgy approach that made the connection. In many ways Sinéad was 'unlearned' despite her connections with the likes of In Tua Nua, Ton Ton Macoute and U2. Up to the age of 15 she was relatively ignorant of contemporary music, confessing on some occasions to a liking for The Cure, The Smiths, Bob Dylan, Van Morrison, Patti Smith and The Doors.

In truth her influences were more random than eclectic. In her own words she was "a complete dildo" who knew "nothing about music" until she was 15. Ironically, though the unfortunate Mick Glossop is the one most often tagged with the charge of comparing her to Grace Slick, it was Grainge and Hill who first told her she sounded like the Jefferson Airplane/Starship singer.

"Grace who?" was Sinéad's reply and she was equally unaware of Aretha Franklin. When Grainge asked her where she felt she fitted into the musical spectrum, she replied somewhere between Kate Bush and Madonna, which just about covered all the stops and any detours.

When the album was released, Sinéad set off with a new band – including The Smiths' rhythm section of Mike Joyce and Andy Rourke – and a battery of behind the scenes electronic wizardry, in support of Australian band INXS.

The tour was not without incident. During a visit to Liverpool, Sinéad and former Smiths' bassist Andy Rourke were involved in a fracas in a hotel disco. The pair were turned away from the disco at Liverpool's Adelphi Hotel, where they were staying, because they were improperly dressed. When they changed and returned they were still refused admission. Then when Rourke made a remark about "needing a dicky bow to get in here" he was allegedly punched in the face. Sinéad intervened by shouting at the bouncer to stop and anointing him with the contents of her glass. She was then punched, according to a spokesman, and dragged across the hotel foyer and thrown down the hotel's stone staircase. The following day she had to cancel a photo call because she was nursing a shiner and some bruises. It was, in newspaper parlance, 'a good yarn' and didn't waste its time in Liverpool. Within a day it was reported in the London *Standard* and Dublin's *Evening Press*.

The British nationals, particularly the tabloids, had thus far ignored Sinéad, partly because she hadn't yet achieved sufficient celebrity status for them to begin prying, and also because her image and music were sufficiently impenetrable to coax anything more than a perfunctory glance out of them. The *Sunday People* did however name-check her in a January feature on the pop faces to watch out for in 1988. *The Guardian*'s Bob Flynn was fulsome in his praise under a review and interview entitled 'Scream Of The Crop', and a tonsil revealing head and shoulder photo of Sinéad that looked as though it had been taken from the Auschwitz files.

Although Sinéad had played support to The Waterboys at a low key concert in Dublin's Olympic Ballroom in May, 1986, her triumphant

"After fighting to keep the baby and going through the pregnancy and labour I felt like, hell, I can do anything I want."

homecoming to Dublin was delayed until March 4, 1988, at the same venue.

The Olympic Ballroom is one of those city venues that has served a thousand purposes – it launched a thousand love affairs and marriages in the showband heyday of the fifties and sixties, served as a bingo hall and roller disco and, in the late seventies, became a venue for the rising stars of the punk and new wave movements. With a capacity of 1500, the polished wooden dance floor is surrounded by red plush leatherette seating and overlooked by a narrow viewing balcony.

On the night of Sinéad's homecoming the weather was mild, a damp, drizzling haze of rain falling in the black Dublin streets. Camden Street, littered with cabbage leaves and fish bones from the day's market trading,

With former Smiths bassist Andy Rourke.

was full of curious young Dubliners swarming to the hottest show in town – the return of a new Irish star. There was a palpable air of excitement and anticipation in the nearby hostelries as lucky punters with tickets got in a last scoop before curtain up.

Inside the hall was seething – packed to the gills, even a shoehorn wouldn't have got anyone else in.

Since the criteria for showbands was to make the dancers sweat, the ballrooms were not designed for air conditioned comfort. The building's own pores had opened that night and perspired into a puddle.

Upstairs at the rear of the balcony an area had been cordoned off for guests and press. Before the band hit the stage the roar from the frenzied crowd was already deafening. Promoter Jim Aiken, a veteran of entertainment promotions in Ireland since the early sixties and one of the most influential in the country, was strolling about backstage, an incredulous look on his face.

"Have you ever heard or seen anything like this?" he screamed in my ear. He confessed to being absolutely flummoxed by the whole affair. Upstairs, above the din, Sinéad's father John and his wife Viola and other members of their family were huddled in groups, smiling and mesmerised.

Sinéad appeared on-stage, black Dr Marten's, black tutu, black tights and black basque. The place erupted, swayed and staggered.

John O'Connor beamed with pride. "Do you like the music?" I

asked him. "I love the music," he replied.

Outside the hall in the evening drizzle ticket touts were doing brisk business – unusual for a show of this size – and according to promoters, tickets were passing hands for as much as £40 apiece.

Sinéad appeared ill at ease on-stage. The show was lacklustre, hampered by the reliance on a Fairlight and backing tapes. The rhythm section of Mike Joyce and Andy Rourke helped to augment the performance with some spirited playing. Most of the material from 'The Lion And The Cobra' was featured. It was not a comfortable show, and it was exacerbated by the physical discomfort of the building and the howling crowd which kept up its unrelenting baying throughout the proceedings. The atmosphere must have been both enervating and intimidating on-stage. Sinéad managed to throw in some new songs, particularly the one she referred to as the untitled 'new song' on the night and which later become known as a thoroughly uncompromising song about deceit and betrayal, 'The Value Of Ignorance'. I noted in a newspaper review that it presented "an optimistic statement of her future strength."

One week before, Sinéad had made her début appearance on Ireland's premier chat show, *The Late Late Show* with veteran host Gay Byrne. "The time that I was the most nervous in my entire life was when I appeared on *The Late Late Show* for the first time," she said later. "The whole idea of being on this programme I had grown up with and meeting Gay Byrne, scared me shitless. I was almost puking backstage before I went on and I was on the verge of tears. I survived that so I'll survive anything." In fact Sinéad survived well enough to launch a broadside against the Tory politics of another guest on the show, zany British TV comedian and disc jockey Kenny Everett.

Joe Falvey, Sinéad's teacher from Newtown, had been sent a pair of tickets for *The Late Late Show* and had met Sinéad's father for the first time in the TV studio. They both agreed to meet the following weekend at the concert in Dublin.

It was a Friday night, the eve of a rugby international in Dublin. "I wasn't sure where the Olympic was and I was meeting Sinéad's dad in some hostelry on the corner as he had the tickets for me. I was late arriving because it was a horrible night driving up from Waterford. I went up to the door of the Olympic – I asked someone where it was – and spoke to Peter Aiken, son of the promoter, and said that I was on the guest list. So I went in, no problem and met John inside. He said let's go and have a drink – he had his ticket and my ticket in his pocket and we didn't have to produce them. So off we went to have a drink. The tickets had a face value of £6 or £7 and as we were passing back at nine o'clock some ticket tout outside was offering £20 a ticket. We were passing by and he couldn't resist it – John had given me the tickets earlier and he asked me for them and sold the two tickets to the tout. Not that he wanted the money but the huge pleasure of selling his daughter's tickets at three times the price. And he no sooner got the money than he handed it to me and said, 'There you are, Joe, that'll pay for your trip to Dublin'."

Chapter Fifteen

Jump In The River

When 'The Lion And The Cobra' took the music world by surprise so did Sinéad O'Connor.

The album quickly camped in the higher reaches of the British album charts and, far from selling the modest 25,000 copies expected of it, began to shift by the bucket load.

In America college radio stations took up this rarity – a startlingly original sound made by a young girl with a shaved head – the starkest contrast to the anodyne, off-the-shelf teenybop pap then being sold for pop music.

Across the Atlantic the record took off, going gold and eventually selling more than one million copies and then winning a Grammy nomination. As her fame grew the demand for interviews grew too. Editors and journalists familiar with her music and her extraordinary appearance spotted a good story.

Sinéad never failed to disappoint. Her story read like some network TV melodrama – the disturbed and abused childhood, the thieving, the 'school for girls with behavioural problems', the death of her mother, the early precociousness, the discovery and the meteoric rise to fame, motherhood, U2 and the IRA.

It didn't take too long for magazine writers to begin to distort some of the information too. In one magazine the old folks' home adjoining Grianan in Dublin's Drumcondra suburb was said to be crawling with rats and echoing to the sound of old women vomiting and moaning. Sinéad was quoted as saying she had been made to sleep on the floor.

Then she spent a year 'busking in Dublin bus depots and pubs', an episode that cannot be recalled by her former band, Ton Ton Macoute. On more than one occasion press biographies released by her record company suggested the band had split up after her departure. This caused them cancelled bookings and endless credibility problems. Ton Ton Macoute still exist today.

Rolling Stone dubbed her a former U2 protégée, which must have really pissed off the resolutely independent O'Connor. For many writers the 'school for girls with behavioural problems' became a 'borstal', implying a custodial stay on the order of some higher authority like a court. This was not true, either, and when the *Irish Evening Press* used a story to that effect from the British *Daily Mirror*, Sinéad's father John O'Connor, a barrister, was swift to demand and receive a prominent retraction from the paper.

Getting Sinéad into an interview situation proved an added bonus for writers seeking forthright controversy – Sinéad lived up to her image as an outspoken and aggressive protagonist. As detailed in an earlier chapter, it was during this period that she began to make her most controversial statements about Irish supergroup U2, and professed her support and sympathy for the activities and aims of the outlawed Irish guerilla organisation, the IRA.

She told the British music magazine *Melody Maker* in June, 1988, "I support the IRA and Sinn Fein. I don't like the violence but I do understand it, it's necessary even though it's terrible."

Later that year she told Barry Egan for *NME*, "The British troops should be withdrawn from Northern Ireland. I don't think the British people should leave; it's as much their right to live there as anywhere else. But the fucking Government should get out and they should take their fucking death squads out with them ... I don't like what the IRA do," she added, "I don't agree with it but I sympathise with it. I have to sympathise with it. If I really look in my heart and think about it, I have to sympathise. I think it's horrible and I'm really frightened by even the fact that that is how I feel ..."

These were damaging and emotive statements, although in the immediate aftermath the emphasis was placed on the anti-U2 statements by the British music press. Sinéad would later attribute the controversy to a misunderstanding arising from a quotation by an American interviewer.

Someone in America, she claimed to Sean O'Hagan of *The Face*, had asked her if she could understand the depth of human feeling that led to two British soldiers being dragged out of a car and killed by a Republican crowd. She was referring to an incident that occurred at a Republican funeral in 1989.

On the occasion she described to the American reporter, Sinéad said she could appreciate the depth of human feeling and anger and oppression that leads to something like the incident, but she had also said it was horrible. She then complained that she had been inaccurately reported and the story had become a 'Sinéad supports the IRA' story. When she spoke to Sean O'Hagan in December of 1989 she made it clear that she did not support the IRA and never had supported them.

"I support the IRA and Sinn Fein. I don't like the violence but I understand it."

There is a danger of this whole issue being lost in a morass of denials and counter denials. Her declared 'support' for the IRA and her ability to sympathise with their actions is impossible to understand for someone who is not Irish, or at least possesses more than a rudimentary or passing knowledge of Irish history.

Irish history, as taught in Irish schools, has always been a catalogue of the horrors of oppression and imperial aggression visited on Ireland by its more powerful neighbour for over 700 years. It is also a catalogue of the struggles by heroic, poorly armed and outnumbered secret organisations to liberate the country from its oppressors. Such is the historic lore upon which the IRA builds its philosophy, purpose and policies.

Understanding this version of Irish history also lends itself to an insidious ambivalence towards the policies of armed struggle – 'the armchair provo' syndrome – but it can also lend itself to a fully legitimate and shared sympathy for Republicanism, a belief that the British presence in Northern Ireland does amount to an occupation and that the resolution of the Northern Irish conflict can only be found in the withdrawal of the British – their Government, their army and their laws.

Fachtna O'Ceallaigh, Sinéad's then manager, is a self proclaimed Republican and a self proclaimed supporter of the causes of Provisional

Sinn Fein, the Republican political movement led by Gerry Adams MP.

Once known as O'Kelly, he changed his name back to its Gaelic original of O'Ceallaigh and at the start of the decade he was fined a small sum when he was charged in a London court for wearing an IRA badge. He grew up in a Gaelic speaking family environment steeped in Irish traditional music. The message on his London apartment answering machine invites the caller to leave a message, in Gaelic. His return to the Gaelic form of his name and his support of Irish cultural causes is grounded in his conviction that Irish culture, music and language is under threat of erosion by circumstance, business and politics.

Such commendable convictions would remain entirely irrelevant if Sinéad O'Connor had not chosen to manoeuvre her way out of her former statements of IRA sympathy by laying the blame at the feet of others, intimating that words and ideas had been put in her mouth.

"I was involved in very complex relationships during that time and I was influenced by the people I was hanging around with. I wanted their approval and I was expressing things in order to get that approval without realising that that's what I was doing. I should not have condoned the use of violence by anyone," she told *Rolling Stone*.

She also blamed her youth. "I was 20 or 21 years of age when I said those things and I didn't have the slightest idea of what I was talking about," she told Q magazine in March last year, "… I never thought of the moral consequences of what I was saying."

Irish DJ Dave Fanning suggested that many of the things she said then were influenced by Fachtna O'Ceallaigh but she replied that it would be unfair to blame anyone for one's own mistakes. Without conceding that what she had said in the past was a mistake, Sinéad acknowledged that she might have considered her statements a little more carefully before saying them in public.

In the summer of 1989 she appeared with Fachtna at a 'Troops Out' rally in Dublin and while she sang 'Irish Ways And Irish Laws', a song which chronicles the history of British occupation in Ireland, to a large crowd of Republican supporters chanting pro-IRA slogans, Jim Kerr of Simple Minds was on a stage less than a mile away singing 'Belfast Child'.

She later told Sean O'Hagan in *The Face*, "I appeared by myself, for myself, singing a song. I'm a Republican in so far as I think the British army and the British Government shouldn't be there so 'Troops Out' seems a logical thing to support. But to be honest with you, I wish I hadn't done that simply because I don't want to be labelled a Republican slogan chanter."

When these anomalies were later highlighted by Eugene Masterson in *NME*, the article in question, 'Nothing Compares 2 U – turns' was greeted with howls of 'foul play' and 'mean spirited journalism', when all it amounted to was a legitimate comment on Sinéad's dramatic about face which she admitted to herself. Of course, Masterson went on to raise the question about who exactly was to be believed – the 'new' or the 'old' Sinéad O'Connor?

It was a question she had begun to ask herself after the initial flurry of publicity surrounding the success of 'The Lion And The Cobra' and the controversies concerning U2 and the IRA that dogged her footsteps throughout 1988.

*Sinéad speaking at the
'Troops Out' rally in
Dublin, August 1989.*

In July, Sinéad made a low key visit to Dublin to appear at a special Nelson Mandela 'Freedom at 70' concert in Dublin's Olympia Theatre to perform alongside a range of Irish traditional and folk acts including The Dubliners, three members of The Pogues, Irish blues guitar legend Rory Gallagher and Christy Moore.

Sinéad dressed for the show in blue jeans cut off at the knees, a white sleeveless T-shirt and the, by then, customary Babygro tied around her waist. She sang a blood curdling version of 'Troy', accompanying herself on a 12-string acoustic, 'I Am Stretched On Your Grave', a song based on a 12th century Irish love poem, and a unique hip hop meets Celtic bop version of 'I Do Not Want What I Haven't Got'. The highlight of the evening, though, was when Sinéad duetted with Irish folk hero

Christy Moore on 'Irish Ways And Irish Laws' against a giant backdrop of the then still imprisoned ANC leader.

Around this time Sinéad further expanded her musical horizons by recording with New York rapper M.C. Lyte. They collaborated on a souped-up, hard-as-nails funky version of 'I Want Your Hands On Me' which was a commercial flop, and Sinéad followed it up with a collaboration with controversial New York performance artist, Karen Finley, whose records are banned in Britain.

Finley recorded 'Jump In The River' with Sinéad. Was it released for shock purposes Sinéad was asked at the time. "No," she told *NME*. "I just did it purely and simply because I wanted to be able to go home and put a record on that had me and Karen Finley on it, for my own amusement."

Sinéad may have found Finley humorous but others have found her performances, at best, an acquired taste in taboo breaking or, at worst, gratuitously obscene. Finley told Barry Egan of *NME*, "I was thinking of the 'Jump In The River' bit. So I decided to do something on 'Jump' which psychologically made me think of 'jump start'; you know, 'get me started'."

Finley's part in the song also deals with male womb envy – 'After my mother washed me and powdered me, I insisted that she masturbate me. You wonder why I've got panic attacks before later suggesting that her lover hates her through her silken panties.'

"If Karen Finley was a man I don't think many men would be offended by it," Sinéad protested to *NME*. "I think people would say how great this person is. But people are shocked when a woman does anything that's in any way sexual, or aggressive, or hard because it's not acceptable. People would like to think they're capable of not being sexist but all people are sexist."

With a million-selling record under her belt, Chrysalis were more than willing to indulge their precocious young star with non-commercial, 12-inch collaborative mixes with New York performance artists and rappers. Sinéad's intended follow-up to 'Jump In The River' was 'The Value Of Ignorance', a song about the psychological violence of personal relationships: 'All those nights with my arse in your face, and your words in my dreams, now I know what the value of ignorance means.'

By the end of 1988 Sinéad had apparently had enough and word of her imminent departure for Paris was widely reported in the British and Irish papers. The year ended with her personal life and her health in turmoil, her own public image misshapen into some grotesque caricature of a venom spitting, aggressive siren who had nothing good to say about anyone or anything.

Sinéad at the Nelson Mandela 'Freedom At 70' concert in Dublin's Olympia Theatre, 1988. Left: With Christy Moore.

Chapter Sixteen

Feel So Different

1989 wrought significant and dramatic changes in the life of Sinéad O'Connor. The New Year found her preparing to take her leave of London, just as she had from Dublin two years before, escaping the pain of broken relationships, the hounding of the British press and a recurring physical pain that dogged and confused her, when news of her Grammy nomination for Best Female Artist came through.

Her father John first heard about the nomination from Sinéad when she phoned him at Dublin's Shelbourne Hotel from London.

"Just to let you know first," she told him, "it seems I'll be nominated for a Grammy." Soon after O'Connor recalled in the *Sunday Tribune*, "As often happened with telephone calls from or about Sinéad over most of her life, I wound up spluttering, in this case from a mixture of pride and pleasure for her."

"I'm very happy," she told her father.

The following Sunday – January 15 – the story was carried in an Irish Sunday paper, and on the same day Sinéad's older brother, Joe O'Connor, had his first short story printed on the *Sunday Tribune*'s 'New Irish Writing' page. Joe, who is three years her senior, was an outstanding honours student of English at University College, Dublin. His first novel and a collection of short stories were published in 1991.

Sinéad headed off to attend the Grammy awards in the glittering razzmatazz showbiz surroundings of Hollywood's Shrine Auditorium. It was a typically perverse twist of logic that Sinéad, the anti-rock star, should delight in such Hollywood showbiz excess.

"I thought it was quite funny," she later told *NME*. "I don't belong in a place like that but I was quite happy to be there because, while you don't belong in a place like that, it's great when people elect you because you realise that people don't always think along the same lines. Like a lot of people say you shouldn't do *Top Of The Pops* because it's just pop, but my attitude is, well, you may as well jump in at the deep end."

She continued this tortuous logic with the belief that, "If you can't beat them, join them but get in there and give them a foot up the ass. That's fine by me. Like there's no reason on earth why you shouldn't go on *Top Of The Pops* and think, 'Listen to this, you fuckers!' Something completely brilliant can get on *Top Of The Pops*."

Sinéad's 'kick up the ass' was delivered to the live Shrine Auditorium and coast to coast TV audience in the shape of a black bra, torn blue jeans, Docs and a Public Enemy logo stencilled into her scalp.

Her fellow nominees in that year's awards were Tina Turner, Toni Childs, Melissa Etheridge and Pat Benatar and the Grammys gave Sinéad their own 'kick up the ass' by awarding veteran war horse Tina Turner the prize for an album few will remember.

A year later Sinéad's gracious memory of the occasion ran thus: "Tina Turner won. May she rot in Hell. Toni Childs, Melissa Etheridge and Pat Benatar were also nominated. I'm glad Pat Benatar didn't win, I'm not a rock and roll chick, that just doesn't appeal to me."

Meanwhile, backstage at the Grammys, Sinéad, in the company of her good friend, the impish Irish journalist and *bon vivant* B.P. Fallon, went meeting and greeting with the rock stars. Dressed in a black leather jacket with elaborately painted sleeves and a T-shirt emblazoned with a portrait of the Virgin Mary, she moved among rock's legends, mouth agape, collecting autographs.

"It was the first time I'd experienced the whole glitz thing," she told 2FM DJ Dave Fanning. "It was nerve wracking. I went around with my eyes wide open and there was Al Green wearing this incredible gold shirt made of wrist watch straps and Stevie Wonder and Little Richard."

Sinéad collected autographs from Andy Williams, Dizzy Gillespie and Quincy Jones, who asked for hers and then had his photograph taken with her for his kids. Later Sinéad met the Reverend Al Green and asked him to bless her and he, in his gold wristwatch shirt in the middle of all those other glitterati of the Hollywood rock set, held her hands and bent his head in silent prayer and blessed her.

Later on-stage she sang 'Mandinka' and there in the front row was Stevie Wonder smiling, bobbing and weaving his head to the song. "This was the best day of my life, ever," Sinéad told Fallon after the show.

Within a month of returning to London Sinéad married John Reynolds, the father of her son, Jake. The two had separated after the birth of Jake. "We'd both been seeing other people but no matter who I went out with, I always had this feeling of emptiness. I'd constantly feel unsatisfied, lonesome," she told Sean O'Hagan. "Then John started seeing this girl I know and that made me feel even more disturbed. I figured out that it was because I still loved him and I really wanted us all back together again as a proper family. It gives me such great happiness, the three of us together that I wish I'd married him ages ago. It's the best thing I've ever done in my life."

Sinéad attending the Grammy Awards.

That March Sinéad was in the basement bar of Fitzpatrick's Killiney Castle Hotel when I ran into her with a couple of her friends. There was a post-Irish music biz awards bash going on upstairs and I enquired whether she was there for that but she said no. She was unaware that it was going on at all. Then she volunteered, with a wide grin, "I just got married." We congratulated her, bought our drinks and walked away.

The following morning I rang her father, my former landlord, to confirm the story of Sinéad's wedding, but he angrily suggested I ask Sinéad. Distrusting my own slightly inebriated recollection, I shelved the story only to see it splashed in Gill Pringle's *Daily Mirror* column three days later under a headline that suggested Sinéad had got married in secret because she didn't want to spoil her hard girl image. This was patently untrue. She had volunteered the information about the wedding to myself and another journalist that night in the Dublin hotel, although her father's reaction to my enquiry the following day seemed to suggest that he was either unaware or disapproving of the union.

Whatever the circumstances the decision to marry was caused by, it precipitated a lengthy period of self examination for the young rock singer. Without an album since the 1987 release of 'The Lion And The Cobra' the music world eagerly awaited the follow-up, the traditionally 'difficult second album'. Evidently Sinéad had other priorities.

"Around the time I got married," she told *Rolling Stone*. "I had been physically ill for a long time. I'd been going to doctors and nobody could figure out what was wrong. Then for a whole summer I saw a woman, who's like a spiritual healer and a dietitian and I started doing yoga with her." That process, she said, gave her a chance to get her act together mentally and ... "to begin to see that I was involved with people who were bringing out negative things in me."

Her persistent illness was unspecified but involved 'very, very serious gynaecological problems' and despite the attention of a series of doctors, no-one could sort it out. "I was very, very sick," Sinéad told B.P. Fallon in the *Sunday Tribune*, "and I was very, very messed up in my head."

Selina Marshall, the spiritual healer and dietitian she attended regularly that summer of 1989, changed Sinéad's diet completely, putting her on a vegan diet without any animal produce, tea, coffee, cigarettes or sweets. It was difficult, she told Fallon, but during that summer she found the strength to follow the regime. The result was a return to perfect health and for the first time, happiness.

"She is the one who is responsible for my happiness," she said, "because even for a long time after I got married I was very sick and I was very fucked up in my head and she sorted me out, so it is really due to her."

Marshall receives a dedication on the inner sleeve of 'I Do Not Want What I Haven't Got' along with another spiritual instructor with whom Sinéad became involved that summer, Warren Kenton. The dedication reads, "Special thanks to Selina Marshall and Warren Kenton for showing me that all I'd need was inside me."

"I realised that I had no control over myself – that other people were in control of me, that I was expressing opinions that were other people's, that practically everything I was doing was to please other people," she told *Rolling Stone*.

Selina Marshall also led Sinéad to the study of the ancient and esoteric science of Qabalah and numerology. She attended a weekend course conducted by spiritualist Warren Kenton. "I went in and it was the most enlightening experience of my life, it changed my life," she said. "The weirdest things happened. It was brilliant. I felt like I could see why I had been born, I could see what God meant when He made the world, I could see that we all have a part to play ..."

Sinéad's visit to Kenton rekindled an old interest in spiritualism that had begun with midnight ouija board parties at school and other such fanciful teenage dabbling.

Sinéad dates it back to the sudden death of her mother in 1985. "My involvement in spiritualism began after my mother died," she told *Select* magazine, "So in a way ... I'm almost grateful to her for dying ... I don't mean that the way it sounds. But if it weren't for her I never would have become involved and never started thinking the way I think, so I feel a great deal of gratitude."

Sinéad also persuaded her mother to take her to the French shrine at

Sinéad O'Connor \ Feel So Different

Lourdes and in her teens harboured dreams and aspirations of being the reincarnation of St.Bernadette, the teenage peasant girl who witnessed the visions at Lourdes.

This involvement with spiritualism also dates back to her days with Ton Ton Macoute, her old Dublin band, whom she would later castigate for their involvement with witchcraft and magic. Sinéad was not averse to soaking up much of the so-called 'paperback wisdom' available to her then and she once offered to read an Irish journalist's tarot on a later visit to Dublin.

Kabbala, Cabbala or Qabalah is, according to the *Collins English Dictionary*, "an ancient Jewish mystical tradition based on an esoteric interpretation of the Old Testament." Its historical usage describes any secret occult doctrine or science and is a cover-all phrase for general magic philosophies. In the words of a Spiritualist friend, "It is the most complex aspect of occultism."

It is drawn from the Hebraic word, 'qabal' which means to receive and when translated literally Qabalah means 'from mouth to ear', an oral tradition and science of learning. In simple terms, using the Qabalah involves an act of personal balancing, both internally and externally. It provides the person with a structuralisation process, an internal filing system that allows them a systematic method of relating to the external world on one hand, and their internal mental processes on the other.

The purpose of any magical practice is to effect change – and such change can be directed internally or externally. The object is to achieve a perfect internal balance through that change.

Many of the current Western trends towards esoteric systems of knowledge have their basis in oriental teachings, where the ancient and mystic wisdoms were never suppressed but have existed and developed alongside general oriental religions and philosophies to the present day and can be found in oriental philosophies of Chi and Yoga.

In the West the suppression of Qabalistic teaching sent it underground where it was covetously guarded by adepts and initiates. It has passed through the ages in Jewish circles and through early Christian sects. Qabalistic teachings have been found in the workings of the Rosicrucians and the Alchemists. All of these secret organisations and philosophies can attract the gullible and the receptive mind. The true knowledge, believers say, is secret only because the keepers of those secrets hold them in trust and are obliged to divulge them only in a responsible fashion. What emerges as Qabalistic teaching today is a mixture of other received notions of Hebraic, Arabic, oriental and Greek origin.

W.E. Butler, a grand old man in English magic circles of this century, has pointed out that occult knowledge has rightly been held secret since what has been revealed in certain branches of say, modern psychology, has been misused and perverted by what he called the 'unscrupulous people' of American advertising agencies.

To the receptive mind, the Qabalah offers a refuge from confusion and a way of relating to the external world and how it affects the individual and Qabalist student in terms of black and white.

In the light of all this, Sinéad O'Connor's intense period of internal auditing in the summer of 1989 goes some way to explaining the new-found serenity and happiness with which she greeted the new decade of the nineties.

But before that time came she began the process of physically changing her surroundings, influences and relationships. "I decided I had to assume control over myself in every aspect and that meant I had to sever some relationships that were very very difficult to sever. I had to summon the strength to say bye-bye to people that I had previously thought I couldn't function without.

"Now," she told *Rolling Stone* in April 1990, "I feel like I'm sitting at the helm, where I'm supposed to be sitting. Now I'm captain of my own ship."

Sinéad began and continued her internal audit with a regime of daily self examination involving yoga, chanting, numerology and the study of the Qabalah. It gave her life a purpose, she said. "I'm more sure of myself now and why I'm here. I like myself more now." This new found sense of purpose also gave her the strength to accept mistakes and experience a new belief in reincarnation and Karmic debt.

"Over the past months I've sat down and looked at everything I've said and done and believed. Some I got rid of and some I kept. But there's no regret. It's like ... you know when you see a photograph of yourself at 15 and you're wearing fucking horrible clothes that you thought at the time were great? So you shouldn't knock what you've done in the past," she told *Select*.

She confronted her image as a rent-a-shocking-quote loudmouth in bovver boots in the snarling, screaming press photos and interviews and discovered that the origins of all that apparent hostility and 'bad karma' were directed at her during the years between the release of 'The Lion And The Cobra' and 'I Do Not Want What I Haven't Got'. The fault, if there was any to be found, lay at her own doorstep.

"I'm not blaming anyone," Sinéad told *Hot Press*. "I can't say it's not my fault because it is my fault. I went around shooting my mouth off about things I had no right to shoot my mouth off about. It's all very admirable to be completely honest and say what you think but now I think it's more important to know what you're talking about and be aware of the impression you're giving. I hope that I can change people's opinion of me in that respect and show that I'm not some tough, brash thug. I have as many insecurities as anyone else, probably more."

Among the least convincing of these personal revisions was her assessment of the visual impact of her former image "I didn't intend that by shaving my head and wearing Doc Marten's and bomber jackets that I would have an aggressive image. It didn't occur to me until very recently that that's the image I had, I couldn't understand why people thought I was aggressive and tough and everything because I'm not really at all," she told *NME*, "but people only see what's in front of them, and unfortunately I went around shooting my mouth off about things because I thought I was the bee's knees, you know. As one does when one is stupid."

In Ireland her image was taken with a mixture of amusement and admiration. While some people may have been prepared to accept the image of wide-eyed, guileless and gullible innocence there were others, myself included, who believed what we heard in 'The Lion And The Cobra' and looked beyond the brash, aggressive image to the romantic

"I had no control over myself... other people were in control of me..."

soul that lurked beneath the veneer. "Her songs are the true image of her beauty, her fears and her resolve," I wrote in a profile of her for the *Irish Press* in March, 1988, shortly before she made her triumphant homecoming to Dublin. The album, I added, was a strong statement of identity from an intensely creative singer and songwriter that almost screams: "I *am* Sinéad O'Connor," before concluding, "'The Lion And The Cobra' has exorcised her demons, the joy of Sinéad O'Connor has yet to come."

One of the most painful consequences of Sinéad's personal rediscovery was the severance of her relationship with long time mentor, manager and friend, Fachtna O'Ceallaigh.

The dismissal when it came was abrupt and sudden. O'Ceallaigh was in Dublin shortly after the break and was said to be in a state of disbelief

and shock. His only comment on the dismissal was published in *Rolling Stone* in June, 1990.

"What is important to me is what Sinéad says," he told the American rock magazine. "She is the one who knows exactly what occurred over the three-year period that I managed her. And even more important than that her reaction means everything to me because she has always been and will always continue to be, as long as I'm alive, a best friend of mine.

"Everything else, whether it's success or fame or whatever, all the things that attend success – it's all basically rubbish. I never thought of Sinéad as a person or object who made records. I thought of her as a human being and friend."

It was a fittingly gracious and heartfelt postscript from O'Ceallaigh, who, true to his own form has remained entirely silent on the subject since.

For her part, Sinéad, has heaped effusive plaudits on the head of her former manager: "I wouldn't be doing what I'm doing now if it wasn't for Fachtna," she told B.P. Fallon in the *Sunday Tribune* in February 1990. "I've huge respect for him and he's been very good for me and very helpful to me. I love Fachtna and he loves me and that's all there is to it." She told *Rolling Stone*, "Fachtna had given me a sense of my rights as an artist. He instilled in me the idea that I must have control over what goes on regarding how my image and work are presented. Most important, he was instrumental in showing me that I should be honest and true and not compromise myself."

Others were a little more forthcoming on their assessment of Fachtna's influence. Her father told *Rolling Stone*, "Fachtna came too close to seeing Sinéad as a possession. Management should be an arm's length affair; there's a relationship that has to be kept scrupulously in its place. The manager's first duty is that their client's career should be maximised and they should not let their personal feelings into it at all – whether they're political feelings or emotional feelings."

Chris Hill, Nigel Grainge's partner at Ensign Records, said, "He did two important things: he helped her discover a part of herself – her sense of purpose and worth – but he also badly fucked her up. And the two things together are what made Sinéad O'Connor what she is."

Ambivalent as Hill's assessment may be, it probably comes closest to the truth when the circumstances of Sinéad and Fachtna's relationship – one that went far beyond the ordinary manager/client relationship – are considered. According to *Hot Press* editor Niall Stokes, "If Sinéad was open and trusting, Fachtna was almost the exact mirror image."

Sinéad with Fachtna O'Ceallaigh.

Stokes described O'Ceallaigh as "defensive and paranoid" and "confrontational" but he shared a fierce sense of conviction and an impul-siveness with Sinéad, and as their professional, artistic and personal relationship developed the two began to have more and more in common.

In retrospect, Stokes believed *Hot Press*'s lukewarm review of Sinéad's début album at that potentially critical juncture in her career led in turn to the artist's strained relationship with the Irish magazine. It was shortly after the release of the album that Sinéad began her vitriolic attacks on U2, and *Hot Press* magazine was never far from her thoughts or utterances in those interviews.

O'Ceallaigh's musical ideology, Stokes argued, was based on the belief that being loud, snotty and obnoxious was essential to rock 'n' roll and may have either consciously or subconsciously transferred these beliefs to Sinéad.

Such a theory is both patronising and inaccurate. It is more likely Sinéad shared these feelings with O'Ceallaigh and it helped to cement their relationship. Sinéad, as her father has pointed out, "has a primeval sense of justice" and hand in hand with that sense of justice went what Stokes called "a fierce hatred for anything that smacked of hypocrisy." She expressed these feelings in bursts of "righteous anger", and the problem was, according to Stokes, "she was frequently wildly off target in her sideswipes."

"You must go through phases and learn from your mistakes," Sinéad told 2FM DJ Dave Fanning. "I didn't think before I spoke."

Sinéad was reluctant in that interview to place the blame for her own views and bolshiness at the feet of O'Ceallaigh. She did admit that often in the past she had spoken out of turn about subjects she was not qualified to speak about. "I said things about them (U2) because there was the whole situation between them and Fachtna, who used to run Mother Records, and he was upset when all that ended. Fachtna was my best friend and I felt hard done by and so I said things. I should have thought about it from their point of view as well before I said things like that and then it all got worse and worse."

Above all, her new spiritual awakening gave her a new confidence in her art, an art that has often been interpreted as extremely emotional and often very painful in its expression. To Sinéad those emotions are intense but not painful. "Art has a specific function which is to reflect spirituality," she told *NME*'s Roger Morton. "I believe very strongly that you choose your life before you're born, that you choose what the whole path of your life is going to be and what function it is you want to perform and who your parents are going to be and all that stuff."

On a higher plane she told Morton she believed that the function of art was to reflect God and all the knowledge gained in another incarnation.

With herself in full control of her spiritual well being, she soon found the perfect man to look after her temporal affairs. Veteran American rock manager Steve Fargnoli appears to have specialised in the expert handling of difficult and precocious artists. Having once steered the career of Sly Stone at a time when no-one would touch him, Fargnoli went on to handle the affairs of Prince before the Minneapolis pocket genius fired him.

Sinéad with Steve Fargnoli, who took over as her manager from Fachtna O'Ceallaigh.

Sinéad met Fargnoli through her old friend, Karl Wallinger. He was a natural choice for her, given that her career was about to take off with the release of her new album she needed someone she knew and could trust to handle the purse strings and do the deals.

"He was the first person I thought of asking because I had met him before and I didn't want to ask some complete stranger and also because he manages Karl Wallinger who is a similar type of artist," Sinéad told *Evening Press* rock writer Roderick O'Connor.

With a new manager, a new album and a new spiritual resolve it was time to face a new decade.

Nothing Compares

To You

If 'histrionic' is the word most often used to describe 'The Lion And The Cobra', Sinéad O'Connor's startling 1987 début, then 'serene' must win the vote for 'Most Frequent Critical Adjective' in relation to the follow-up, 'I Do Not Want What I Haven't Got'.

From the soft focus John Maybury cover, a spotlight on the serene gaze in Sinéad's blue-green eyes, to Sinéad's recitation of the Serenity Prayer by Reinhold Neibhurr that opens the album, 'I Do Not Want What I Haven't Got' clearly signals the change that had come about in Sinéad's life and art.

"I was 20 when the first album came out and I thought that I knew everything about everything and I thought I was great. But I realise that I wasn't great at all now I'm 23. It isn't much older but you develop through your life, and your reasons for doing things change.

"You stop being so introspective and you start thinking about other things in life," she said in January 1990, the same week that 'Nothing Compares 2U' was released, the chartbuster single that heralded and heightened anticipation for the album's release later that spring.

The album's first song is the prayerful 'Feel So Different', whose literal title signals the source of Sinéad's new found peace and serenity, presumably gained from her summer of holistic treatment and meditation. It is a liberating experience gained from her internal psychic excavations – the source of her strength, she sings, against a slowly gathering tempest of strings, is within herself.

It is followed by 'I Am Stretched On Your Grave', one of two songs, including the Prince penned 'Nothing Compares 2U', not credited to Sinéad. 'Stretched' is drawn from a 12th century Gaelic poem and celebrates the ancient Gaelic practice of mourning, when a widow would lie or sit on the grave of her dead husband or lover for a proscribed time. The poem was translated from the original Gaelic by the Cork born short story writer and playwright, Frank O'Connor, and included in a collection of his translations published in 1962. It was in turn read and put to music by Phillip King, the Irish TV producer, musical archivist and blues harmonica player with Irish jazz and rock combo, Scullion.

The song still exists as a 'sean nos' Gaelic song in Ireland entitled, 'Ta Me Sinte Ar Do Thuama' or, literally, 'I Am Stretched On Your Grave'. King wrote the music as true to the 'sean nos' (shan nose) style (a unique Irish traditional a cappella style) that translated means 'old style or way'.

According to King, "Sinéad O'Connor sings that song the way she does and only Sinéad O'Connor can sing it that way because she is Irish and because she knows how to sing it in this style." Her treatment of the song is all the more remarkable for the use of a beat box and tapes and traditional fiddle playing by former Waterboy, Steve Wickham. The song is a unique weaving of the new and the old, the hip hop and the sean nos and in many ways, from the song's evocative love story to this crazy mixture of styles and traditions, it sums up the genius of O'Connor.

Then to 'Three Babies' and the theme of an intimate journey through Sinéad O'Connor's soul begins to focus and unfold. Feet shuffle and people begin to scratch themselves when they hear this track. They look around for somewhere to plant their eyes and put their feet and hands. While 'The Lion And The Cobra' could draw primeval instincts of violence and fear from a listener, 'Three Babies' will make you squirm.

"It sounds like an emotional song," she told *NME*'s Roger Morton, "but it's just thinking about emotional things that happen to you from a spiritual point of view." Her answers to direct questions about the song have always been evasive. Remarkably, when Sinéad sang the song on Terry Wogan's BBC TV show in November, 1990, Wogan asked her if she wrote all the songs from personal experience. She hardly hesitated, blurting 'yes' before biting her tongue as the TV host missed the opportunity for another of Sinéad's almost compulsive confessional outbursts.

So to 'The Emperor's New Clothes', wherein Sinéad's tongue lashes music business hypocrisy, the record company people who tried to have her abort her unborn child and who, presumably, drove a wedge between her and her husband John Reynolds, causing them to split up for a period after Jake's birth and the release of her first album. "This business is very cynical," was a common refrain of Sinéad's throughout 1990. "When the press looked at me they saw a woman with a shaved head and a pair of Doc Marten's and they assumed I was strong, rough and aggressive. It really hurts when people think that. It can hurt so much I feel like crying," she said, and here she sings how she will go and buy herself some new clothes sometime, but not until she has said her piece.

'Black Boys On Mopeds' is the only song that strays from Sinéad's policy of writing from personal experience, although the song, wilfully naïve political analysis included, is the album's first indication that Sinéad's mind was opening up to events that surrounded her.

That primeval sense of justice her father wrote about in 1989 is once more evident here, as the song deals with the case of Nicholas Bramble, the Ladbroke Grove youth accused of stealing a moped loaned to him by a friend. In the ensuing chase Bramble crashed and died.

The album also carries a dedication to Colin Roach and his family. Roach died from gunshot wounds received in the foyer of a London police station. An inquest concluded that Roach shot himself in the entrance to Stoke Newington Police Station, near a flat where Sinéad once lived. There have been numerous calls for a full inquiry into Roach's death. His father was awarded £12,500 damages against the London police for unlawful arrest during a Colin Roach protest march in 1989.

"I live around here and I can't help but see how badly black people are treated," Sinéad told *The Face*'s Sean O'Hagan, "Same as America. Treated like pieces of shit. Mind you," she added, "anyone who isn't English is treated like shit."

Much has been made of the celebrated tear shed by Sinéad in John

Maybury's marvellous video that accompanies 'Nothing Compares 2U'. There are almost as many interviews quoting Sinéad as saying the tear is 'acting' as there are ones where she protests its authenticity.

"I didn't intend for that moment to happen," she told *Rolling Stone*, "but when it did I thought 'I should let this happen.' I think it shocks people. Some people, I know, really hate it – maybe because it's so honest or maybe because they're embarrassed by displays of emotion."

Director John Maybury almost thanked 'the plate of onions' when he accepted the MTV Award for the video in Los Angeles in September 1990. In the March 1990 issue of Q magazine, Sinéad told Mark Cooper the tears were 'acting' but added, "Acting isn't pretending. It's using your past experiences, summoning them up to tell a story that's not a lie but the truth." In the December 1990 issue she told Adrian Deevoy, "They were real. Too fucking real. John Maybury … was going to thank the plate of chopped onions at the awards and I'm glad he didn't because everyone in the room, including him, was in shreds when we made that. We were all in a terrible state. It was very upsetting. That was the first take and it all came out."

She also gave an insight into the cause of the tear. "I was fairly fucked up already, I was under enormous stress, I'd just split up with my manager (Fachtna O'Ceallaigh) literally two days before we made the video so my life was really falling apart. It was all quite apt, I felt pretty ghastly. Also it's a pretty heavy song. 'Don't Worry, Be Happy', it isn't, you know?"

The song, a cover of a song Prince wrote for Minneapolis band The Family, had never been recorded by Prince himself and the original, sung as a duet, trading choruses, sounds half finished and petulant in its delivery. O'Connor's treatment of the song gives it its transcendent and poignant angst. The song's painful lament and barrel of turbulent emotions struck a universal chord. Technically difficult to sing, her treatment of the song is one of the greatest 'cover song' hijacks of all time.

Its commercial impact – selling a million copies in England in one month after its release and becoming one of the fastest selling solo singles of all time, before later topping charts all over the world and hitting the top of the *Billboard* Hot 100 at almost the same time as the album – took them by surprise.

"If you think about the kind of songs I write it's strange that they would be commercial. I mean, they're so personal. I think about why I wrote a song like 'Last Day Of Our Acquaintance' and then I think about millions of people buying and listening to it … it's really weird," she said.

Whether, as they have said, the massive success of 'Nothing Compares 2U' was unexpected – "I knew it would do well but never dreamed it would do that well," Sinéad told one journalist – the packaging, marketing and timing was perfect.

It even prompted an attempt by Prince to reclaim the song which he never recorded himself, adding it to his set list for the 1990 European tour, and releasing a commemorative greatest hits album for promotional use only which he cheekily labelled 'Nothing Compares 2 Him'.

Inevitably, Sinéad and Prince met. The relationship was friendly at first but soon ended in a night of acrimony and terror with Sinéad accusing Prince, the ultimate rock egotist, and a man who liked to dress his female backing singers in lacy lingerie, of jealousy. More seriously, she accused the Minneapolis based star of holding her against her will and threatening to beat her up.

"I think it would be fair to say that I dislike Prince profoundly," Sinéad told Helena Mulkearns of *Hot Press* in December. "His problem was that I did a song of his without him being involved in it. He's jealous. And he did say to me that he wished I'd never done his song, so fine, I'll never do it again. I think frankly that the song saved his fucking ass. He was in serious financial trouble until that song happened."

It appears Prince lectured Sinéad about her national anthem outbursts and her own cursing. Then in the course of an argument in the American star's home at 5.30am, Sinéad began crying while Prince refused to give her a lift home or tell her the number of a cab company – he said he didn't know his own address.

Prince, "apparently unaware of his own address."

"What I object to is that if he had an argument with me, that's fine, but I don't see why he had to threaten me with physical violence, and use the fact that he is a man to intimidate me and be quite amused by the fact that I was frightened," Sinéad said. The episode appears to have drawn the final curtain on any future performances of 'Nothing Compares 2U' or any other Prince-penned covers.

It was released as a single in January, 1990. A press release issued by Chrysalis's London press office in December signalled the imminent release and invited applications for interviews. It also made tantalising mention of a film, *Hush A Bye Baby*, in which a bewigged Sinéad would make an appearance.

This was a second bite at the cherry which had gone seriously sour for the young singer two years before, following the release of her début album and the subsequent magazine storm that blew up around her and her outspoken tirades against all and sundry. Few were pushed about taking up the offer of the interview … until they heard the single and saw the video. It was instantly recognisable as a potential monster hit.

"Absolutely spellbinding and haunting," I wrote in my own Irish press rock column the day following its release. I was convinced beyond a shadow of any doubt that this song was destined to top charts everywhere.

Dubbing her "the mad princess of melancholy" the *NME* singles' reviewer called it "the first great love song of the nineties" and later called Sinéad "the first superstar of the new decade."

It is hard to believe her record company were not aware of that too. They were certainly aware enough to allow almost three months to pass before the release of the album – and by that time the Sinéad O'Connor rollercoaster was gathering pace fast. Interviews were only granted with a guarantee of covers. Sinéad entered every interview with her own tape recorder – this time she was going to get it right.

No other single released from the album has achieved anything like the success of 'Nothing Compares 2U' and it is likely the record company was aware this would happen. 'Mandinka' was an unexpected success on the début album but no other single released by Sinéad has made any impression on commercial singles charts, not that she has expressed any desire to make such an impression. Quite the reverse, in fact.

So did the tear in 'Nothing Compares 2U' sell six million copies of 'I

Do Not Want What I Haven't Got'? Hardly, but it didn't do any harm, acting as it did as a marketing, text book-style teaser to draw those consumers unfamiliar with the product into its warm and mysterious embrace.

'Jump In The River', the track that follows 'Nothing Compares 2U' is vintage 'bolshy' O'Connor, the 'Paddy With Attitude' singing a song about obsessive, devil may care, love and lust, complete with hammering beat and grungy guitar. This was one of the songs she had released before as a single and the one she made with controversial New York performance artist Karen Finley.

Sinéad has consistently refused to talk in any detail about her own songs but the lyrics are there for people to read and explore. Her life is here and there, laid out in interviews and books, like a microphone placed in a confessional. Sinéad is very aware of the influence of her mother on her music and it is likely the song 'You Cause So Much Sorrow' is about her, a presence Sinéad has felt around her since her mother's tragic death in 1985. "The songs," she told Sean O'Hagan, "are about where I'm at and they unfold chronologically so there are still a few, er, slightly angsty ones at the start of the record."

"It is simply a record about a 23-year-old human being and what she makes of her experiences. Some of the experiences are angry and some are hurtful," she told *Rolling Stone*. "I write about whatever it is I happen to be going through at the time, so if something awful was happening to me that's what I wrote about."

One person close to both Sinéad and Fachtna, who declined to be interviewed for this book, did say in reply to a question about the possible cause of why Sinéad dispensed with the services of Fachtna O'Ceallaigh, "I wouldn't have an idea but my feeling about how any of that unfolded and ended has to do with the attraction between two extremely strong willed people. This should not be taken out of context but whatever happened I would hate to be the guy who Sinéad wrote that song, 'The Last Day Of Our Acquaintance' about."

Ensign boss Chris Hill says he was shellshocked when he first heard the album. "It's so personal, we couldn't even make a judgement about it and we couldn't think in terms of whether it was a hit record. It is intense."

"Nigel and I had both been through divorces," he added. "You listen to some little girl singing 'The Last Day Of Our Acquaintance' and you know what it's about. We've been there."

Sinéad was concerned that Hill and Grainge's reaction to the album might be to refuse to release it. "Nigel told me," she recalled, "'You can't put this out; it's too personal'," to which she replied, "People that like me, like me because of that. That's what I do."

"I know she thinks it's a happy record," Hill remarked, "but it doesn't convey happiness – it conveys trauma. Because of our reaction she thought we didn't like it and she said, 'It's not for men to like, it's a woman's statement'."

"I know some of them (the songs) sound very moody," she told Liam Fay for *Hot Press*, "but these songs were all written during my current phase of contentment and happiness. They've none of the introspection that dragged some of my earlier songs down. They're celebrations, affirmations of life. There's very little sadness in them."

"I think it would be fair to say that I dislike Prince profoundly."

Sinéad O'Connor \ Nothing Compares To You

And so the title track, 'I Do Not Want What I Haven't Got' closes the album and marks the end of Sinéad's extraordinary journey from unhappiness to happiness. It's a traumatic gauntlet, fraught with those personal demons and pitfalls she is now prepared to confront. But if the closing song is meant to convey contentment, it is a restless or conditional contentment. Although in the song she is advised not to become too pure, it's not enough for our girl … "Ultimately I want to be the purest creature in the whole world," she would say later.

On stage at the Hammersmith Odeon in May 1990.

The reviews for 'I Do Not Want What I Haven't Got' were, for the most part, ecstatic. Some tempered their enthusiasm with a little caution, particularly Irish and English reviewers who remained suspicious of Sinéad's volte-face and expected at least one bare-faced, naked scream of vitriol from its tracks or at least from her in person.

David Quantick, giving the album a credible '8' in *NME*, called it, "a controlled, intelligent and even tidy album" adding, "It's also pretty good." But he remained circumspect about the "constant emoting", the abundance of the singular person 'I' throughout the tracks, "the inconsistent politics toss", but as he concluded, "When it's done as well as this, who cares? 'I Do Not Want What I Haven't Got', is a truly fine and smart set of songs, an original and imaginative album."

The Irish *Hot Press* magazine, whose 'fair' (lukewarm) assessment of her début was later regretted in print by some of its writers, particularly Bill Graham who subsequently reviewed the new one, gave it a '10' out of a possible 12 which meant it fell into their 'exciting' grade.

Graham noted the disparate elements on the album – hip-hop, new wave, Celtic singing, bleak, rock ballads – that appeared to find coherence only in Sinéad's singing. Graham noted how the album was far less the 'prayerful' album spoken about in interviews and far more a chronicle of the struggles endured to achieve this new found state of grace. The album might be egocentric and self important, he noted. It might not find too much favour with the over 25 male set but it was nonetheless 'special', he almost apologetically asserted.

'Nothing Compares 2U', he noted, had by then already been accorded the supreme accolade "sung by the female freemasonry on the last bus" but he singled out 'Three Babies' and 'Feel So Different' for special mention too. The album, he observed, was "spare and monochrome, very much the product of a London exile who'd immersed herself in hip hop and tenaciously refused to let her vision be clouded by any acid house technicolour." Here he spotted how Sinéad had merged the Gaelic sean nos with hip hop, in a marriage that might have sounded forced and unnatural but which worked because its bleak setting ridded it of any "sentimental trad associations".

Comparing Sinéad's work with that of veteran Irish author Francis Stuart, both – "stubborn, stumbling, wayward spirits prone to headbutting truth in their youth" – he noted that they shared a common fear of not expressing the intensity of their emotions. 'I Do Not Want What I Haven't Got', he concluded, was "an unflinchingly brave testament and conclusively, the first major Irish album of the new decade."

Robert Sandall, writing for *Q* magazine accorded the album four stars out of five – an 'excellent' grading where the five star or 'indispensable' is only very rarely granted. Under the block capital headline of 'SHIMMERING', one of those words along with 'cascading word-

sounds' usually reserved for self conscious Cocteau Twins' reviews, Sandall tackled the thorny issue of overt influences and concluded that O'Connor "serves brilliant notice that originality in the 1990s is as much a question of interpretation as of invention."

Veteran *Time* magazine staff writer Jay Cocks drew an interesting, insightful and flattering comparison between O'Connor's music and that of Van Morrison, both being Irish and both given to using their music as a vehicle for self examination and psychic speculation, a telling comment given Sinéad's own acknowledgement of Morrison's influence. "He makes me want to write spiritual music," she once said.

San Francisco Examiner pop critic Barry Walters described the album as "not a collection of songs but an exploration on a theme: loss" and concluded that this was music of a rare grace and vulnerability and the product of a woman with the will to explore her deepest, tenderest emotions. "'I Do Not Want What I Haven't Got' is the LP that proves great albums are still possible," he concluded.

American reviewers were, in general, far less restrained about O'Connor's second album. Mikal Gilmore, the author of the most comprehensive O'Connor interview in print in *Rolling Stone*, drew comparisons with Dylan's 'Blood On The Tracks' and John Lennon's 'Plastic Ono Band' for being "intensely introspective" and "so affecting and farsighted, it seems capable of defining the mood or experience of an entire audience."

But even as the plaudits were being heaped upon the single and the album all over the world, closer to home storm clouds were gathering.

Chapter Eighteen

I Do Not Want What
I Haven't Got

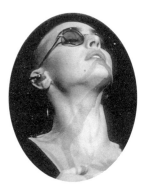

The storm clouds and portents were there from the start. Under the head-line, 'Beginning To See The Light', NME's January 13 cover story carried a caveat in the subtext: "Can it be true?" they asked. "For two highly successful years she was all leather, lather and lip, the undisputed queen of verbal violence. Maybe a bit barmy too. But now with her second LP on the slipway, SINÉAD O'CONNOR has grown up, calmed down, tuned in and cooled out. So she reckons anyway. Having heard her motormouth merrily through religion, revolution, reincarnation, Romanians, razor cuts and Axl Rose, however, we're not so sure …"

In *The Face* Sean O'Hagan's interview had been conducted in the London flat of her then manager, Fachtna O'Ceallaigh, but less than a week later he noted Sinéad had sacked her manager and the record company asked if all references to him could be expunged from the interview as 'irrelevant'.

In an unprecedented editorial comment on the title page of the popular style bible magazine, it was noted that in an issue where picture approval had been demanded for features on Janet Jackson and Keifer Sutherland, the magazine had refused to allow Sinéad O'Connor to see the copy in advance of publication, arguing that "somewhere between the sensationalism of the tabloids and the censorship of over protective publicists is the truth" and that, they argued correctly, "is something worth fighting for." In the light of the sensational events that were soon to unfold in the ongoing soap opera of Sinéad O'Connor's career, particularly relating to her principled stands on the issue of censorship, Sinéad's initial forays into the print interview jungle were marked by their demands for cover features as barter, and the exclusion of certain subjects from discussion, particularly her former manager.

Sinéad set out to perform a massive press campaign and hopefully shift attention from the less adult and unhappy Sinéad who had made 'The Lion And The Cobra' and said nasty, bolshie things about U2 and the IRA. More than shift attention, she aimed to explain her position and demonstrate how changed she was. To make sure that this message was correctly perceived and received, she brought along her own tape recorder to each interview, "to learn and improve my technique of communicating" she told one reporter. Sinéad was not going to be 'manipulated' by the media again into saying nasty things about U2 or anyone else.

In Ireland the rock press was also lining up to interview the country's latest superstar, where, despite their own self-generated hype, real superstars, apart from U Know Who in one league and Hothouse Flowers and Enya in another, were thin on the ground. Sinéad, despite her Dublin background, was still an unknown quantity at home, having more or less disowned the Irish scene for London.

A series of interviews had been lined up for Saturday, January 27, the week her single had first topped the Irish and British charts. Although *Hot Press* magazine had already run an extensive cover story/feature interview on her, there was intense competition among national newspaper writers to 'scoop' the story. Behind the scenes digging and string pulling was being carried out to get a telephone interview in advance of her visit, or else secure the inside story on the split with Fachtna O'Ceallaigh, a well known figure in his own right and a very newsworthy local story.

Eleanor McCarthy, head of the Chrysalis Records' office in Dublin, and a highly experienced and respected publicist and marketing manager for her label's clients, was well used to these machinations and she was equally determined to dole out the interview opportunities as democratically as possible. I was one of the journalists who was working hard to get 'the story' and perhaps unwisely and over-zealously I made enquiries about Fachtna to people who were too close to Sinéad O'Connor and caught up in the prevailing paranoia. On January 26, the day before the intended interview, which had been confirmed by courier to take place at 11.30am, Saturday January 27, at the Shelbourne Hotel, I received an apologetic phone call from Eleanor informing me that the interview would not now take place. After further enquiries I was told it was because I had been ... "prying, ringing her (Sinéad's) friends and trying to get her home phone number."

Ah! My heinous journalistic crimes were laid bare before me in their full brazen horror. My reaction was one of disbelief. Surely Sinéad O'Connor could not be party to such blatant censorship. I decided to fax off a missive direct to her hotel in the hope of turning the situation around. Anger and indignation got the better of me.

Here is what I wrote, marked "Attention: Suzanne Parkes (Chrysalis press officer)/Sinéad O'Connor ... Your decision to exclude me from the scheduled interview list is at least misguided and at worst, an injustice. Surprising, coming from someone who is perceived for their commitment to justice and fair play. On the other hand, not so surprising since the artist appears to have fully embraced the star making ethos that involves ego massage, censorship and revisionist attitudes.

"Assuming that I, like any working journalist, should have done my homework, there are questions that are best raised than left suspended, unanswered. Once the question is asked, a refusal to answer is acceptable. However, assuming that you had done your homework, you should be aware – however superficially – of my track record as a journalist. I do not set out with preconceived notions before an interview nor is the piece written until after the interview. For the record, what mention I have made of Sinéad O'Connor in the past has been positive.

"Sinéad is fond of talking and writing about her spirituality and peppered her first work with numerous religious references, not least 'The Lion And The Cobra's' title. My own meagre acquaintance with things biblical recalls a phrase ... 'Judge not lest ye be judged' ..." It was an angry, ill advised sliver of melodrama, the kind she relishes and I regret. It almost, according to people there on the day, prompted an angry telephone reaction from Sinéad. Ten months later in Dublin's Baggot Inn she attacked me for sending her 'nasty letters'.

That night she appeared on Irish television's most popular chat show, *The Late Late Show*, and charmed the show's host by turning his own puckish bravura on himself. "The last time you were on the show," he told her, "I got the impression you took a bit of a shine to me, Sinéad."

"I thought it was the other way about," Sinéad replied, stopping him dead in his tracks.

It was a brilliant performance by her. She was lively and affable. She sang 'Nothing Compares 2U' and then answered calls from listeners. Asked about her position on the IRA, she disingenuously but deftly parried the question by implying she had been misquoted by an English tabloid newspaper, a reply sure to garner sympathy from an Irish audience.

Sinéad appearing on the Late Late Show, February 1990.

Journalists who were granted interviews were told Sinéad was very tired and had been really busy in the previous two weeks with considerable demands being made on her time. She was surviving the deluge of attention on coffee and cigarettes. Added to all this was the recent trauma of the split with Fachtna.

Evening Press rock correspondent Roderick O'Connor, who was well known to O'Connor from previous interviews, remembers Sinéad was tired looking and though friendly, was initially unresponsive. She livened up as the interview progressed, eventually answering questions about her former manager that went a little further than what had been known until then.

Evening Herald rock columnist and feature writer, Eamonn Carr, didn't fare so well. Carr, a rock and roll veteran himself, having served his time as drummer with Irish Celtic rockers Horslips throughout the seventies before embarking on a career as an independent record producer, promoter and pioneer hip hop and rap DJ, had just got off a plane from Moscow when he was dispatched to the Shelbourne Hotel. A student of spiritualism and karmic debt himself, not to mention an avid fan and promoter of dance music, Carr felt he shared a few interests with Sinéad. Unfortunately he met a monosyllabic and uncooperative Sinéad, tired, drawn and wary. Carr left early complaining there was little of interest on his tape and certainly not enough for an interview. His features editor thought differently and prevailed on him to write a piece which highlighted his complete dissatisfaction with the entire conduct of the meeting.

For Sinéad too much was happening too quickly. She could feel her life changing and worried that it might never be the same again. "In the beginning I was completely freaked out," she told Adrian Deevoy of *Q* magazine. "By the time 'Nothing Compares 2U' happened I was almost in a state of shock. I was zapped mentally anyway from all the trauma of the album and hassles in my private life. I wasn't eating properly, just drinking coffee and smoking hundreds of cigarettes and getting totally stressed out." Her problems with the Irish press were nothing compared to the baying British press hounds. The first tabloid salvos were tentative – Jonathan King in *The Sun* had declared himself a Sinéad fan but *The Sun*'s pop columnist, Piers Morgan, dug up the Sinéad O'Connor supports the IRA angle from two-year-old music press cuttings and the then current spate of revisions from Sinéad in the music press. After four weeks at the top of the British singles chart, suddenly it was open season.

Ironically it was an article in *NME* written by an Irish journalist that appeared to set the whole thing alight. The *NME* ran a story by their Irish correspondent, Eugene Masterson, entitled 'Nothing Compares 2U – turns' wherein he proposed that Sinéad O'Connor's stand on so many things had changed so dramatically in the first couple of months of 1990 that it appeared as though she had cashed in her radical bolshiness for a stab at the big time. In the process, the article implied, she had ditched her manager and acquired a new one better versed in the politics of image making, and done a crash course in media manipulation on the side.

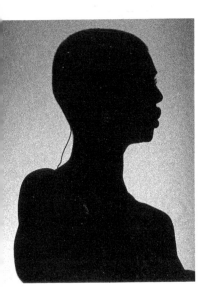

My own position vis à vis Sinéad O'Connor was dragged into the whole argument and Masterson, with my permission, quoted from my rock column of the week following the interview that never happened. My position was clear, I wrote, "No-one can deny her the right to change, whether it's her views, hairstyle, her music or her management. But no-one should try to manipulate how that image is perceived by the public or deny anyone the right to ask why." In the event my newspaper, the *Irish Press* was not denied the right to an interview, only me, and a substitute was arranged to take my place. In retrospect I regret the pressure placed on Sinéad O'Connor during that time, but journalists believe if someone can't stand the heat they should get out of the kitchen. Sinéad O'Connor may have been treated insensitively by some Irish journalists but only because we felt we had been treated insensitively by her or those surrounding her. There was, and still is, an enormous amount of goodwill towards her in Ireland but she has never seemed willing to either appreciate it or exploit it.

Sinéad came to Dublin in mid-February to fulfil a long-standing engagement and perform at the Irish Recorded Music Association (IRMA) awards in Dublin's Point Theatre. The programme was broadcast live in front of over 6,000 young fans and stars like Chris de Burgh, Clannad, The 4 Of Us and Sinéad O'Connor were lined up to perform on the night. U2 manager Paul McGuinness also accepted an award on behalf of the band for their 'Outstanding Contribution To The Irish Music Industry'.

What should have been a triumphant homecoming for Sinéad was probably more like a nightmare. She shunned photographers and jour-

nalists who mingled with the performers and music industry personnel in the venue's spacious 'green room' backstage, and when she made her way off-stage along the backstage corridors to her dressing room, she looked tired, worried and intimidated.

When the *NME* issue hit the streets on February 17, everything else hit the fan. A whole pack of reporters and newshounds awaiting scheduled interviews at the Chrysalis head office on February 22 were greeted by the white hooded figure of Sinéad disappearing, head down, along a record company corridor clearly upset. They were told the article had upset Sinéad and she was unable to carry on with any interviews.

Tim Nicholson of *Record Mirror* was there that morning. Sinéad later phoned *Record Mirror* cancelling all interviews, explaining the reason being "the unduly rough treatment she had received from the press, both pop and tabloid." Nicholson then went on to point out *NME* writer Eugene Masterson's 'other job' as a reporter for the *Irish Daily Star*, a paper that is half owned by the British tabloid *Daily Star*. With this revelation he then proceeded to analyse the avalanche of negative tabloid press stories that had descended on the singer in the previous fortnight.

Despite Masterson's other job and the allegedly "scathing and mean-witted piece of journalism", what he had done in that *NME* article of February 17, according to *Rolling Stone*, was to raise the issue of credibil-

*On stage at Brighton
Conference Centre,
April 1990.*

ity. Music writers were well aware of Sinéad O'Connor's past views on the IRA and U2. When Sinéad reappeared in the public view with a new album, manager, hairstyle and a whole new bag full of opinions, people had to decide which Sinéad they should or could believe. It was therefore legitimate practice to query the credibility of her obvious about turn and the reasons behind it.

In the circumstances Sinéad was ill prepared, unable or even unwilling to answer many of the questions – she expected people to accept her changes at face value and when they weren't she was prepared to brand the doubters as 'cynical' and 'manipulative'. On some occasions she acknowledged her own share of the blame in her previous U2 and IRA controversies, but then intimated in other interviews that she had been manipulated and should not share the full brunt of the blame. She tied herself up in her own knots.

Were the music papers perpetuating a lie by trying to discredit the reinvented Sinéad O'Connor or should they have accepted the change and presented the new serene Sinéad to their readers as a *fait accompli*?

Sinéad had told journalists that she had a habit of treating interviews as 'a chat in a pub' or 'intimate exchanges between friends', unaware that being in the public eye required her to be a little more circumspect in her views and less inclined to shoot her mouth off.

Rock stars have never been averse to talking about themselves – why not? It's part of the process of selling records. In the eighties more than any other time, though, the rock star has been queried on a wider variety of issues, ranging from population control to censorship, starvation, poll tax and, in Sinéad's case, the IRA.

There is a dilemma here – rock stars are citizens like anyone else and are just as entitled to their views, but does a chart success or a new album give a pop star a mandate to speak on such issues in the context of a pop music interview? Are they really in a position to influence anyone? And why is it that among celebrities (other than politicians) it is only rock stars who are subjected to this kind of interview. No-one asks England cricket captain Graham Gooch or soccer superhero Paul Gascoigne their views on world events, nor are actors and actresses judged according to their political opinions.

On the other hand, what right does a music journalist have to solicit such opinions from a rock star? Does the search for 'good copy' have no bounds in this context? Where interviewees are obviously game to shoot their mouths off, does that give the journalist the right to exploit a tendency which might just be manifest naïvety? Whipping up publicity with some well turned epithets, slags and headline-grabbing stunts is as old as rock and roll itself. Any aspiring rock star must keep a well turned set of opinions and positions on a huge variety of subjects about their person if

Sinéad O'Connor \ I Do Not Want What I Haven't Got

they want to pursue that route these days. If they don't – and shoot their mouths off with opinions they later choose to refute in horror – then they have clearly been misguided, ill advised and badly informed.

Sinéad O'Connor doesn't sing protest songs or songs about the ecology or the IRA. She sings about herself, her emotions, her life. She sings about these subjects with a startling and painful – even brutal – honesty. Why she sings about such things in the way she does is a legitimate subject for discussion. Because she chooses to sing about such subjects, she raises questions in the minds of her fans about who she is. How genuine are her feelings as expressed in her songs? Fans who identify with her through her songs want to know more about her. What they identify with are those emotions so painfully and honestly expressed.

If Sinéad's personal life was in turmoil when 'Nothing Compares 2U' was launched upon the world, then why was she being presented to the world at that time as a serene, happy, wife and mother? There is another point. Sinéad O'Connor is an intelligent person with strong opinions on a variety of subjects. If she wishes to express those opinions she must accept the consequences that those opinions, once expressed and published, become public property and are open to further comment, quotation and question.

Whatever her problems with the music press, the British tabloids turned their attention to her when she became such a runaway success in the British singles charts. Frustrated by Sinéad's refusal to entertain any requests for interviews, the British popular papers turned to the music press for their information and it didn't matter if the story was two years old. To them, everything was 'recent'.

On February 3, the *Daily Express* ran a feature entitled, 'MY SHADY PAST, NO 1 GIRL SINÉAD'. The article was a complete rehash of all those other stories about Sinéad O'Connor, well known to music press readers familiar with her over the previous two or three years, but news to the majority of *Daily Express* readers.

By February 15 the *Daily Star* were whipping up their own head of O'Connor steam with a story built on a remark she had made about Terence Trent D'Arby. The following day the *Daily Mirror* and *The Sun* both ran stories with different pictures about Sinéad's former job as a kissogram girl – a story well known to music press readers for more than two years. In the hands of the tabloids it became a 'big secret' and a 'saucy secret'. Not only had the chart topping feminist and anti-sexist made a living as a kissogram girl dressed as a French maid, she had enjoyed it. Aaaarrgh! It was time for the big stories to come out, the major profiles, the interviews, the centre spread features. The *Daily Mirror* was first with 'Nothing Compares To Being A Mum' by David Hancock on February 20.

Three days later at the San Remo music festival Sinéad was reported to have 'outraged' Italian hoteliers by walking barefoot across the lobby of the plush Hotel Londra. The comments from the hotel manager were less than outraged.

When the album was released in March it quickly took up a perch at the top of the British album charts. It was time to raise the ante on this girl who was laying claim to celebrity status in showbiz writers' diaries and who was obviously not going to go away. Marcus Berkmann, reviewing the album in the *Daily Mail*, remarked how stardom in pop music could beckon without adequate warning.

The album, he concluded, was a fascinating curate's egg, "a hugely varied mish-mash of different styles and approaches that's both painfully personal and a brave attempt to stretch rather than cosset the unsuspecting listener." Two days later in the *Daily Mirror* on March 15, an article on Sinéad's dedication to Colin Roach, the young black man who died from gunshot wounds in the foyer of a London police station, was accompanied by a note that Sinéad was no stranger to controversy. As if to underline her moral turpitude, the paper recalled her stint as a kissogram girl, and her "spell in a rehabilitation centre for shoplifting" as well as her former support for the IRA.

One week later the *News Of The World* added further 'evidence' to this insidious catalogue of veiled racism with a story headlined, 'SINÉAD'S SINS WITH HER MARRIED MINISTER', a story culled from an excerpt in an interview with *Spin* magazine writer, Legs McNeil, about Sinéad's affair with a married London preacher when she was 17.

By May Sinéad had saved the fortunes of Chrysalis Records and the company was insuring her for £1 million.

In June things began to take a sour turn. First she cancelled shows in Glasgow, Edinburgh and Newcastle, scheduled between June 19 and 21 after she collapsed with exhaustion. Meanwhile the *Daily Mirror* had discovered how … "Her joy at the worldwide success of her bitter sweet music is tinged with deep sadness – Sinéad still grieves for her estranged mother, Marie." On June 26 the *Daily Mirror* dropped its bombshell.

Under the headline 'Nothing Compares To Hugh' the paper revealed how Sinéad had left her husband for 25-year-old Hugh Harris, the support act on her US tour. It was noted that Hugh Harris was a 'black' rock singer and Sinéad had deserted the father of her three-year-old son Jake, only a month after telling *Rolling Stone* she was very happy in her married life.

Sinéad headed back to America amid a flurry of rumours about her relationship with Harris after turning up with him for former Pink Floyd man Roger Waters' extravagant performance of 'The Wall' in Berlin on July 22.

But the land of the free was no safe refuge.

Sinéad at the 'The Wall' concert in Berlin, July 1990.
Right: with 'Wall' composer Roger Waters.

Chapter Nineteen

Star Spangled Banner

With life in London turning into a nightmare for Sinéad, the embrace of America offered welcome relief.

The increasingly intrusive UK tabloid media now reported that she was pregnant by her new lover, Hugh Harris, and soon after that announced that she was in danger of losing the child.

Within two weeks of their American release, 'Nothing Compares 2U' and 'I Do Not Want What I Haven't Got' both shot to the top of the *Billboard* albums and singles charts.

"These are the kind of things we expect from a Michael Jackson or a Bruce Springsteen or a Madonna," said Greg Thompson, senior director of pop promotion at Chrysalis Records. "For an artist of unfamiliar name to accomplish that is really something." Thompson should have learned his lesson from the début 'The Lion And The Cobra' which had been expected to shift no more than 25,000 copies and sold a million. On that occasion marketing people in Chrysalis' US office had said they would shave their heads if the album became a success and Sinéad duly turned up with a razor to perform the ceremony. Chrysalis executives took a full page ad in *Billboard* sporting bald wigs when the album went gold.

As Gary Graff of the *Detroit News And Free Press* said, "The 23-year-old singer's success is a study of the hip ascending to mainstream tastes. It's been accomplished through persistence, smart marketing, timing, the element of surprise and lest we forget, sheer talent." No-one, he wrote, apart from Sinéad herself, could take the credit. Thompson believed the single was a special and unique record, the kind that don't come along that often.

'Nothing Compares 2U' happened in America with consummate timing, just as it had done in England. "It was an unusual sounding record in a period of time when music had gotten really kind of boring," according to one Top 40 FM station programmer. "We went for quite a while looking for records that were something different and when this one came it was BOOM! It sounded different on the radio and it was emotional. It just hit home." If Sinéad was unprepared for what had begun to happen in England, she must have been shellshocked by America.

There celebrity status puts you on the list of tourist attractions, loony fan mailing lists, death threats and the cover of *Rolling Stone*. The latter she achieved in June. On May 12 she turned down an invitation to appear on America's top rated *Saturday Night Live* when she discovered the show would be hosted by controversial comedian, Andrew Dice Clay. "I feel it shows disrespect to women that *Saturday Night Live* expected me to perform on the same show as Andrew Dice Clay," she said in a statement issued through her New York publicist. "It would be nonsensical of *Saturday Night Live* to expect a woman to perform songs about a woman's experiences after a monologue by Clay." Clay was already notorious in America for twisting nursery rhymes into obscene anti-female polemics. By November Sinéad would change her tune again, telling chat show host Arsenio Hall that if she had the choice again she would appear on *Saturday Night Live* since she disagreed with censorship in any form.

In Houston, Texas, a radio station decided to offer free tickets to anyone who agreed to have their hair shaved on a rooftop overlooking the freeway. Madonna had just been through the town on her 'Blonde Ambition Tour' so they dubbed Sinéad's tour, 'The Bald Ambition Tour'.

Similar promotions popped up everywhere she went. "In America, people are obsessed," Sinéad told an Austin, Texas, DJ. "It's really, really shocking. It's so frightening. They follow you around and it freaks you out. Anything could be happening, what am I supposed to do?" In America rock stars are celebrities and fair game for the promotion and fame game. As one promoter put it, "We do that to everybody," while another said, "I'm sure it probably bothers her. I've listened to her album and it's a really serious, artistic piece. But the fact that she has short hair and the fact she's very unique opens up the joke pile." Following what had occurred on her return to Europe that summer and what had happened during her one month mini-tour of the United States, Sinéad was already voicing her reservations about the fame game. "When I finish the show," she said, "I'm off duty. I don't want to be intruded upon. It's no wonder that people end up on drugs or drink. People treat you as something which isn't real." On her return from the Berlin Wall show in July the *News Of The World* had a centre spread feature about her efforts to contact her mother by seance after feeling a spooky presence and strange occurrences in a flat in Maida Vale. The chronology of the story suggested the incident had happened some time before and involved some dabbling with a ouija board. The *News Of The World* cobbled together remarks Sinéad had made in a *Spin* magazine story referring to her continual obsession with her mother.

The nanny, Martina Langer, revealed how the two had dabbled with a ouija board on a mirror marked with lipstick.

This was nothing compared to the paper's revelation the following week that Sinéad was pregnant by her new lover, Hugh Harris, and had celebrated by breaking the news to both John Reynolds, her husband, and Harris. Twelve days later *The Sun* reported Sinéad had dumped her new lover after a succession of blazing rows on the second leg of their American tour. Four days later Sinéad cancelled a concert in Cincinnati after complaining of stomach cramps, immediately the tabloids had it turned into 'FEARS FOR SINÉAD'S BABY', reporting that 'the temperamental star' had told her record company, "I'm fed up being treated like an animal and sick of fame. People are always hassling me and none of it has anything to do with me as a person or as an artist." Sinéad's depression reached its lowest ebb at this point. She told *Rolling Stone* in October, "They (the press) really insulted me as a person and continually made me out to be some sort of real bastard. It used to really hurt my feelings. I'm not the most secure person on the planet, you know. It's very very difficult to deal with being seen as a celebrity by practically

"I'm fed up with being treated like an animal and sick of fame. People are always hassling me... and none of it has anything to do with me as a person or as an artist"

everyone you meet. I like the fact that a lot of people like my records but I don't like being famous." Having cancelled a number of shows in Britain in June, Sinéad was well enough to play the Glastonbury Festival, a giant three-day open air festival that raised funds for the British Campaign for Nuclear Disarmament and which had become a rallying point for the burgeoning New Age movement. Sinéad headlined the Saturday night at Glastonbury and, according to one writer there, "Embodied the fiery, dark, absurd poetic legacy of Ireland" far more than other Irish bands like Hothouse Flowers or U2.

She played Belfast Opera House the following night and Dublin's Point Theatre before a seated crowd of 6,000, the night after that. It was Ireland's first glimpse of the 'I Do Not Want What I Haven't Got' live show.

Her support act and rumoured lover, Hugh Harris, put in a lacklustre display, before an audience totally unfamiliar with Harris' rather moody, sombre music. On-stage he had difficulties with his backing musicians and the indifference of the audience gave the whole setting an air of unreal tenseness.

Above: performing at the Glastonbury Festival.
Right and following page: on stage at London's Royal Albert Hall, November 1990.

Sinéad appeared on stage against a stark, even austere backdrop for the opening song 'Feel So Different'. Then a burst of acid rainbow colour greeted 'The Emperor's New Clothes'. There followed a short set that was warmly received and which was, by turn, indifferent and stunning. Her motions switched with the mood of the material, from balletic to jerky, just as the backdrop colours – related, perhaps, to Sinéad's interest in colour therapy – suited the mood changes.

It was a riveting performance, if just for the sheer, teetering edge, and riskiness of it all. An awkward dancer, her own self consciousness on-stage is used as a defiant weapon in her hands, feet and body. One minute she's a whirling dervish, the next, demure, shy, angular.

She closed the show with a trilogy of 'Nothing Compares 2U' – tense and intense – 'Jerusalem' – awesome – and 'Jump In The River', which was manic. And in the prevailing World Cup football fever no-one shouted 'more' just 'Olé, Olé, Olé'.

She returned to the stage and launched into the first major disaster of the evening, the long, rambling Scottish ballad, 'Anachie Gordon', popularised by another Irish singer, Mary Black, whose more sedate delivery and vocal style is better suited to it. In the circumstances of the home-coming frenzy surrounding Sinéad at the Point, it went down as well as a funeral dirge at a wedding. As though to redeem the *faux pas* it was followed by a spellbinding rendition of 'Troy', a solitary performance – Sinéad, guitar, the audience and God.

Returning to America, Harris was dismissed from the tour following a series of bitter rows. The story filtered back to the British tabloids who lapped it up. It was live soap opera, perfect tabloid copy.

"It's nobody's business," Sinéad told *Rolling Stone*. "Why should I discuss what I've gone through with millions of people? I go through a lot of pain and a lot of really hurtful things and if I talk about them in public it causes me a great deal more pain. It doesn't just stop when the thing is printed in the paper. You've got to live with the result of it for weeks and weeks afterwards." She claimed, rather fancifully and inaccurately, that Irish journalists considered her … "The most disgraceful adulteress they could possibly have" having moved, she said, from considering her a goddess just a few months before when she was number one, to criticising her for being famous. They are hypocritical and racist, she alleged.

In reality Irish newspapers had largely ignored the Hugh Harris affair, knowing very little of him or the unfolding events, and none referred to him in those veiled racist tones of 'a black rock singer'.

Mary Glennon, writing in the *Evening Herald* did ask why Sinéad "after praising marriage … is going solo again?" "Every few years a new Sinéad seems to emerge," she wrote. "Which is the real one? Is she just a silly, ill-educated young girl who does her belated growing up very publicly? Or is she a very mixed up person emotionally who is being manipulated by business people far cleverer than she in the ways of the marketing world … maybe now after so much public growing up she will realise that despite her undoubted talent, what she is doing is branding herself as naïve, immature and very vulnerable." Sinéad's concern with how she was being reported at home emerged when my own report in the *Irish Press* about her outburst to *Rolling Stone* stated that the alleged racism was attributed to Irish people in general.

This she promptly denied via a phone call from Los Angeles to another Irish daily newspaper. In this report she explained her *Rolling Stone* remarks: "At the time of the interview I was angry with certain members of the Irish media who were continually prying into my intensely personal and most intimate private life, causing me a lot of pain and sorrow in order to sell newspapers. I said it because I was angry." But as Mary Glennon had pointed out, "Sinéad O'Connor (had) made

"It's very difficult to deal with being seen as a celebrity by practically everyone you meet. I like the fact that a lot of people like my records but I don't like being famous."

the mistake of talking too much about her emotional life. In making it the gospel according to Sinéad and presenting her philosophies with as much earnestness as though they deserved to be carved on stone tablets, she had only succeeded in illustrating the trademark of the young know-all who has quotable quotes on every subject, despite knowing very little about anything." What Mary Glennon was missing here was that all the controversy amounts to the grist for Sinéad O'Connor's creative mill "What I do is I sit around and I think and I get over it, then I look at it objectively and I can see what I learned from it and then I write about it." The pain or joy of experience, the experience itself, is the essence of Sinéad's art. Mind you, despite her traumatic past, that font of experience is still a relatively shallow well.

Shortly after the *Rolling Stone* interview Sinéad walked into the biggest controversial storm of her career.

On Friday, August 24, she was scheduled to play the Garden State Arts Center in Holmdel, New Jersey. Shortly before the show opened Sinéad requested the 'Star Spangled Banner' not be played before her performance. The venue authorities, the Garden State Parkway Authority, acquiesced in the face of 9,000 fans and a performer who was willing to withdraw if the US national anthem was played. The venue authorities subsequently slapped a lifetime ban on O'Connor.

The following night Frank Sinatra played the same venue and told the audience 'He wished he had seen her so he could kick her in the ass.' On Monday the story, and a picture of Sinéad, was splashed across the front page of the *New York Post* under a full page banner headline, 'IRISH SINGER SNUBS U.S.'. Inside, reporter Cathy Burke wrote, "The national anthem – massacred in a recent rendition by Roseanne Barr – gets no respect at all from the shorn locks, Irish singer Sinéad O'Connor. The pop singer flatly refused to go on-stage at the Garden State Arts Center in Holmdel, New Jersey, if the national anthem was played beforehand. A nervous backstage crew – worried a last minute cancellation would cause trouble with a near capacity crowd of 9,000 on Friday night – caved in to her demands. But if O'Connor won the battle she lost the war with New Jersey." Burke went on to report how the Garden State Parkways Authority later decided to slap a lifelong ban on the artist. Burke also mentioned a lack of response from Sinéad's publicist and no explanation from the singer for her action.

In this light, the response by Shock Ink, Sinéad's New York publicist, released after the *New York Post* story, was interpreted as a reaction and an exercise in damage limitation.

That day *USA Today* quoted Sinéad as saying, "I don't see what national anthems have to do with me or my music or my fans" adding that she "didn't mean to be disrespectful" but wouldn't perform after any national anthem, even Ireland's. The report quoted Sinéad as saying she had not been aware that the Garden State Arts Center played the national anthem as a matter of routine before every show there. The paper also quoted Sinéad's objections to arts censorship in America. "I feel very strongly about censorship," she was quoted as saying, "and I don't want to go on-stage after the anthem of a country that's arresting people and harassing people for expressing themselves on-stage." The full text of Shock Ink's statement issued for immediate release that day read, "This was not meant as a snub of Americans. I sincerely harbour no disrespect for America or Americans, but I have a policy of not having any national anthems played before my concerts in any country, not even my own, because they have nothing to do with music in general. I am concerned though, because today we're seeing other artists arrested at their concerts and threatened with having their albums taken off the shelves, or not even released at all. There is a disturbing trend towards censorship of music and art in this country and people should be alarmed over that far more than my actions of last Friday night." The statement went on, "I also want to make it clear there were no complaints whatsoever from the audience, only from the venue management. I was unaware at the time that the Garden State Arts Center was a government owned building and I wasn't told when the date was booked that the anthem would be played. In fact, I was only informed about their intentions to play it 10 minutes before the concert began. Though I would not have gone on had the anthem been played, I was expressly asked not to leave and the G.A.C. fulfilled my request. If my request was so upsetting to them, I wonder why they were so acquiescent to me at the time." The incident occurred in an atmosphere of rising patriotism and war preparations in the United States, due to growing tensions in the Middle East following the Iraqi invasion of its neighbour, Kuwait.

"It was not," as someone pointed out, "a good time to be messing with the flag or the national anthem." Sinéad's statement also served to fuel the row rather than abate it.

While attempting to appease Americans by stating her action was a matter of principle she applied anywhere, even her own country, she also aligned her action with the current censorship debate. This deliberately kept the issue alive.

But the second half of her statement carried a number of inconsistencies – if her policy not to have national anthems played before her shows was such a rigid dictum, why was it not included on the contract 'riders' for her tour? That way both she and the promoter, and the venue the promoter was booking, would have known well in advance of the show that there might be a difficulty.

It is naïve to assume the venue 'acquiesced' to her request. Sinéad O'Connor shows were among the 'hottest' concert tickets in America in the summer of 1990. For the venue authorities to walk out before the show and declare to 9,000 fans that the show would not go on because Sinéad wouldn't let them play the national anthem, might have amounted to suicide.

In the event the story became world news and once more Sinéad O'Connor, the *enfant terrible*, was making the front pages. "That really got exaggerated," she said later. "People went way over the top about it but fuck them. I'm not sorry and I'd do it again in a second. I will not go on-stage after the national anthem of a country which imposes censorship on artists. It's hypocritical and racist." In the ensuing fallout, Sinéad's records were yanked from Top 40 station playlists, although, as Elaine Shock, Sinéad's publicist, later pointed out, "A lot of these stations have only played one song of hers – 'Nothing Compares 2U' – which is basically over as a hit anyway and then banned her. Then they go declaring themselves 'Sinéad free radio'." A Westchester County New York State Senator, Republican Nicholas Spanos, called for a boycott of her Saratoga Springs concert a few days later but no boycott occurred. O'Connor herself donned a long haired wig to mingle with fans and view the protests outside the venue. Funnily enough, she was approached by a local TV news crew, who didn't recognise the disguised singer, looking for reactions from the crowd.

The entire flap about the national anthem also carried the subtext of a recent controversy surrounding TV comedienne Roseanne Barr and her rendition of the national anthem prior to a baseball game in July. On that occasion she sparked off a storm of protest by screeching the song while holding her crotch and then spitting demonstratively after her performance.

Even Sinéad's father got in on the act – asked for his reaction he suggested Sinatra was too old to lift his leg to kick anyone, while Sinéad tellingly replied, "I wouldn't be the first woman he has threatened to hit." Once again, on the night of the show at Saratoga Springs, New York, August 30, the *New York Post* was there and this time ran the headline, 'SINÉAD SAYS SHE RESPECTS AMERICANS'. This time Sinéad made a brief speech to the audience and thanked them for their response. "I am very touched by your reaction to everything you've been seeing on TV and reading in the papers. You were very fair," she stated before launching a bitter attack on a local DJ who had branded her a fascist on the air. She said she was going to sue. The DJ was fired the following day.

The whole story turned out to be a less than nine-day wonder. It was, in newspaper parlance (and happening when it did during the news doldrums of late August), 'a good silly season story'.

One week later a beaming Sinéad swept the MTV video awards in a glittering Hollywood awards ceremony, walking away with three awards for 'Nothing Compares 2U' as best video, best female video and best post modern video.

She beat Madonna and Janet Jackson along the way.

Sinéad at the MTV Awards in Los Angeles, September 1990.

The Last Day Of Our Acquaintance

There had to come a time when Sinéad would be faced with a choice – leave them or join them.

Although she has often protested her loathing for the star trap, of not being a star and not having any wish to be a star, she *is* a star. And that's why she's moving to Los Angeles.

"That's why celebrities hang around together," she told Q magazine, "because they can't communicate with anyone else. When you're a celebrity, another celebrity is the only person who will treat you like a normal human being." Following the MTV Awards Sinéad rented a house in the Hollywood Hills where ... "There's trees and flowers and there's bluebirds and deer outside my house ... everything you want: countryside and five minutes away, the city and then the seaside. It's so stimulating sensually and you're exposed to every aspect of human nature from extreme poverty in one part to the huge houses in another. For someone like me, it's a good place to be in order to learn things." OK, OK, the cynics will scoff at this last remark because now she's living in a human zoo, an urban wildlife park and from her perch she can share experiences with a couple of million other Californians.

Living in California has its own logic for Sinéad O'Connor, the reluctant star who is most at home being a celebrity playing at being ordinary. If she was truly ordinary, no-one would know her. It's one of those paradoxes that chase her about, just another one of those contradictions.

Before taking her leave of Britain, Ireland and Europe Sinéad played one final show at London's Albert Hall. Reviewers noted the strong contingent of lesbian wannabes at the show, crew-cut women in Dr Marten's with grim faces and hunky shoulders. Neil McCormick, reviewing the show for *Hot Press*, was as mesmerised by her voice as he was "annoyed by her hypocritical contradictions", drawing attention to the fact she once tried to take the tape from him after the worst interview of his life (his words).

On MTV, he railed, she turned into Sally Field before our eyes, while the parting line in 'Black Boys On Mopeds' makes him want to shout, "Pack your bags then!" He gnaws at her cryptic obtuseness on 'Mandinka' and, frustrated, demands who is Madame George? Well it's a line from a famous Van Morrison song, Neil.

Finally he relents and acknowledges something we will all slowly realise; Sinéad O'Connor is unique, her music is different, her vision is somewhere else, focused on an otherworldly spot beyond our mortal vision. And 50 years from now, Sinéad O'Connor will still be playing the Albert Hall and packing them in.

Surrounding the show, Sinéad found time to guest on a few chat shows – *Wogan* and *Jonathan Ross* on the BBC and Channel Four respectively. On the latter – she was the first guest of his new show – she nervously smoked a cigarette and joked how her manager was really happy every time she got a new boyfriend.

Then she made another appearance on Ireland's *Late Late Show*, her third in two years. This time the welcome was slightly frosty and she was plied with questions about the American national anthem controversy, for which she had a well rehearsed answer, delivered in that deadly serious, low register monotone she adopts that signals 'brain at work, autopilot engaged'.

"I would find it difficult to step on-stage after the national anthem of Ireland since I, as an Irish woman, am not allowed to have an abortion and I'm not allowed to have a divorce and I'm not even allowed to have a lot of control over my body as far as contraception is concerned. It's a violation of my rights as a human being." In the following days people were divided in their loyalties – many find common ground with her 'right on-ness' on such issues while secretly harbouring a distaste for her chiding attitude – as though she has just discovered these injustices and drawn them to their attention. This would be a misinterpretation of her intentions, though.

O'Connor identifies with victims and once she discovers a new injustice, it's as though it never existed until she appeared.

So a visit to Chile for an Amnesty International show in September 'changed her life'. "I resent the fact," she said, "that this was happening and I never knew about it. I resent the fact that there were concentration camps where people were tortured for their political beliefs up until March of last year and I had no idea about it." When rock celebrities were elbowing each other for the limelight at the Mandela Wembley concert in the summer of 1988, Sinéad was on a smaller stage in Dublin.

Christmas that year she performed at a Nicaragua Solidarity benefit at London's Hackney Empire. Two years ago she said she wouldn't do an Amnesty benefit because they didn't recognise political prisoners in Ireland. Then she appeared at an Amnesty show in Chile with Peter Gabriel and Sting. On-stage the depth of her passion for her new-found cause is palpable in her performance and her fumbled attempts to light a candle for Pinochet's torture victims. She identifies with the Mothers Of The Disappeared. She wants to teach her audience who have come to boogie.

Sinéad is full of contradictions and they are her strength, for in her resolution of those is the spirit of her art.

In the summer of 1990 she threw herself into the Red Hot and Blue AIDS project, an imaginative collaboration of rock singers, directors, performers and fashion designers to construct a TV programme and record to raise funds for AIDS research. It features various contemporary artists performing Cole Porter songs. Sinéad sang 'You Do Something To Me' at the launch in front of a 23-piece orchestra in London's Whitehall Banqueting House. The show was broadcast on December 1 – it featured Sinéad in a blonde wig – and for a whole week leading up to that day, Sinéad presented five shows on Channel Four in their AIDS Update series, delivering her lines in that same deadly serious monotone she reserves for such occasions.

Sinéad, the reluctant star, dreams of what it's like to be on *Top Of*

"When you're a celebrity, another celebrity is the only person who will treat you like a normal human being."

The Pops and practises her Oscar acceptance speech in front of her bedroom mirror.

"I don't want to be a rock star," she continues to protest but Ensign's Chris Hill is not the first person she has told, "I'm gonna be the biggest star there's ever been." Some people believe she is capable of giving it all up.

Below, left: Sinéad with other members of the **Red Hot And Blue** *AIDs project and, this page, singing at the press launch, April 1990.*

Following pages: On stage at London's Royal Albert Hall, November 1990.

Chapter Twenty One

My Special Child

Sinéad ended the year the way she began – controversially.

In a flurry of interviews, TV appearances and a startling, naked 'Mother and Child' study for the cover of *Hot Press*, Sinéad ensured she would not be easily forgotten in 1991.

She told Arsenio Hall how her record company put severe pressure on her to have an abortion in 1987. She told *Esquire* magazine how her mother had beaten her and she claimed to *Hot Press* how Prince, the person who had penned the song that began the year for her with a monster hit single, had threatened to beat her up.

1990 was an incredible year for her. Her records were heaped with accolades and awards. She swept the MTV video awards, beating stiff opposition from Madonna. In a survey of 80,000 teenage American girls her version of 'Nothing Compares 2U' was voted 'favourite song of the year'. Ironically, Madonna topped the poll as 'coolest female musician' and Sinéad was hot on her heels as runner up.

Although an unlikely rivalry at first sight, Madonna and Sinéad have become America's most popular female rock stars.

One dresses as a blonde bimbo and makes love to religious statues. The other shaves her head, wears bovver boots and pretends she's St. Bernadette.

One simulates masturbation and orgy sex on-stage, the other dances stiff Irish jigs with a tape recorder.

They're about as alike as Laurel and Hardy but they probably have just as much in common.

Madonna, the virgin-whore rock star who put the 'raw' in raunch, and Sinéad O'Connor, the androgynous 'Bambi in bovver boots' could almost be twins.

There is an immaculate connection. Madonna named her recent album 'The Immaculate Collection'. Sinéad was born on December 8, the Catholic feast of the Immaculate Conception – the feast day of the conception of Christ's mother without Original Sin.

BOTH lost a parent when they were young. Madonna's mother died when she was six. Sinéad's parents split up when she was eight. Her mother died in a motor accident when Sinéad was 18.

BOTH were raised by a strict, disciplinarian parent.

BOTH were raised in strict Catholic households.

BOTH feel a need to exorcise their guilt through their music.

BOTH are fond of provoking controversy.

BOTH use the media of sex and love, guilt and passion as the central theme of their music.

BOTH have strong religious beliefs and use the imagery of their Catholic upbringing in their work.

BOTH have sought love in the arms of father figures and are drawn to disastrous and destructive relationships.

BOTH are prone to sudden changes of image.

BOTH have a strong desire to feel in control.

BOTH have compensated for a lack of love and affection as children by seeking approval on a wider, global stage.

That feeling of loss from losing a parent when they were young has left them both with a sense of guilt and a desire to gain love and approval.

"I've always wanted to be famous," says Madonna, "for the very obvious reason that people want to be famous because they want to be loved. I guess somewhere along the line when I was a little girl I didn't feel loved." To draw the analogy out even further, those same teenagers that voted Madonna the coolest female musician also voted her 'the uncoolest female movie star' and Madonna, despite all her success as a pop singer, is determined to be an actress.

Sinéad O'Connor shares a similar ambition. "I want to be an actress more than I want to be a singer. I want to be a brilliant actress. I want to be the best actress in the world," she told B.P. Fallon.

In 1989 she was invited to write the score for a low budget TV film by the Derry Film and Video Workshop in Ireland. *Hush A Bye Baby* dealt with the thorny and painful subject of teenage pregnancy in a country where, in recent years, one girl has had a baby in a field and been tried for murder and another teenage mother died, along with her child, in a religious grotto.

The latter incident also inspired a song, 'In The Middle Of The Island', which Sinéad sang with Irish folk singer Christy Moore on his album 'The Voyage' – a singer Sinéad has described as an inspiration and a role model to her.

Sinéad was invited to write the music because of her own experience as an unmarried teenage mother and she readily agreed to be involved. Then her manager Fachtna asked the producers if it would be possible for Sinéad to perform a bit part in the film. She had in mind the role of the Head Nun but it was decided she was too young to play that part. Instead the producers realised they hadn't cast the fourth of the four schoolgirl pals.

The part of 'Sinéad' a demure, devout teenager who has bedroom fantasies of saintly piety is another side of the real Sinéad O'Connor, the little schoolgirl in the boarding school who always longed to be at home, wanted to be a normal person, 'to be accepted, allowed in and treated like a normal human being'.

In the film she wears a cheap brown wig and her performance, as the friend of the girl who becomes pregnant by her boyfriend, though awkward and self conscious is nonetheless courageous. She threw herself into the film work, taking a flat in the northern Irish city of Derry with her son Jake for three weeks and before long, according to a member of the cast, was 'speaking like a native', in the sharp, lilting brogue of Ireland's north west counties.

The music in the film was strangely appropriate, mixing tense, melodramatic cathedral sounds with gentle and genial dance tunes and haunting versions of church hymns – such as 'Ava Maria'. The film ends with 'Three Babies', her own painfully autobiographical song from 'I Do

"I want to be an actress more than I want to be a singer."

Not Want What I Haven't Got'.

That initial introduction to the world of cinema gave Sinéad sufficient confidence to try out for the role of the young tinker girl in *The Field*, the latest film by the *My Left Foot* production team, Jim Sheridan and Noel Pearson which stars Richard Harris, John Hurt and Oscar winning actress, Brenda Fricker.

However, she failed the screen test. "I've been fairly interested in doing some acting for a long time now," she told one interviewer. "I'd nearly become a full-time actress if I thought I was good enough – but at the same time I don't want to be like Roland Gift. I had been offered a couple of parts – there was one in particular in Ireland but I failed the screen test for that and my ego took a bad bruising." The part of the young gypsy girl was won by an unknown Irish actress, Jenny Conroy, spotted, in Hollywood fairytale fashion, in the corridor of a Dublin theatre by producer Pearson. However, Sinéad needn't have felt too downhearted: Joely Richardson, daughter of Vanessa Redgrave, also failed to get the part.

One year later Sinéad's ego has been sufficiently buttressed for her to rekindle her dreams of silver screen fame. Her move to Hollywood will facilitate that and she's already considering taking acting tuition.

Her music must be prepared to take a back seat for now. Sinéad OConnor is an artist who writes from and about her personal experiences and, although she has said her next album will be a very raw and painful one, it is to be expected. In music she is destined to turn a mirror on her soul and turn her sorrow into her art.

In the meantime, once more like Madonna, she seeks the acclaim of a real Movie Star – whether it's dressing up as Veronica Lake, platinum blonde wig and all for the video of 'You Do Something To Me', the Cole Porter song she sang for the 'Red Hot And Blue' AIDS project, or as 'Sinéad', the prudish and reticent teenager in *Hush A Bye Baby* – she seeks to become her own fantasies. "Acting can be an even more powerful medium for getting a message across," she has said. "I think I'd

Sinéad in Hush A Bye Baby with (left to right) co-stars Cathy Casey, Julie Marie Reynolds and Emer McCort.

like to play roles where I could draw from my own personality rather than having to become another person, because I don't think I'd be good at that," she told Marcelle Clements in *Esquire*.

"I'm so used to expressing different elements of myself that it would probably have to be something like that. But I wouldn't do musician things or anything like that. I think the more melodramatic the better.

That's what I like, the old stuff, like *Wuthering Heights* … I fancy myself as … I want to be Kathy (in *Wuthering Heights*), I want to be Scarlet O'Hara (*Gone With The Wind*), I want to be St.Bernadette." If an actor is an empty vessel to be filled by a chosen character, Sinéad O'Connor may have too many characters in her wardrobe to make room for any more. On the other hand she has amassed so much experience in her short and often painful life, that she has a wealth of characters to draw from.

There are more experiences to be lived through. Sinéad must still resolve the conflicts of her own life in further episodes of rigorous and therapeutic self examination. In 1990 she became a world famous rock star. Now she says she doesn't want to be a pop star any more.

"No, absolutely not. That's not the kind of artist I am, luckily," she said in Esquire. "Otherwise I'd never be taken seriously. Who gets taken seriously that puts out a number one record? I'll tell you. No-one, that's who."

Epilogue

As the last sun of 1990 set on the Pacific Ocean, lighting the hills of Hollywood overlooking Los Angeles, Sinéad O'Connor must have breathed a sigh of relief that she had soared the heights and plumbed the depths of the star machine and emerged, relatively unscathed, from the turmoil.

Then the Gulf War began

OK, so it seems a little far fetched to link such an event of world shattering importance with the fate, career and ambitions of a 24-year-old rock star. But if magazines and tabloid newspapers were willing to give Sinéad's attitude to the Star Spangled Banner front page and network news coverage, then she would use their facilities to get her own message across.

The Irish humorist Brian O'Nolan, who wrote under the pen names of Flann O'Brien and Myles Na gCopaleen, once said with his tongue planted firmly in his cheek, "James Joyce is an artist, he says so himself." Sinéad O'Connor says she is an artist and with such assurance and understanding, her duty is clear.

Sinéad's opportunity to shed the shackles of stardom, make her point about the Gulf War and reach some people who might begin to understand what she has been doing, came in February, 1991, with a triumvirate of music award ceremonies - the American Grammys, the British Brits and the Irish IRMAs.

The story first broke in the *Los Angeles Times* on Friday, February 1, in the form of a letter from Sinéad to Michael Greene, chairman of the US National Association of Recording Arts and Science, the body that runs the Grammy Awards. That weekend it emerged she had sent similar letters to the chairman of the Irish Federation of Phonographic Industries and the chairman of the British Phonographic Industry.

They read like manifestos for truth and anti-commercialism, outlining her belief that an artist's function is to be truthful, to inspire, guide and heal the human race. Organisations such as the NARAS, the IFPI and the BPI are too concerned with the commercial achievements in 'art', she said. They celebrate commercial achievements in their awards ceremonies. They were not alone.

"A lot of artists," she wrote, "have been responsible through our work, for making material gain look like a doorway to happiness for the human race. The human race is homeless - it is abusing its children - it is starving - it is stopping itself from expressing itself. It is killing itself and the earth which is its Mother. The human race is at war, because it loves material success and because it does not love itself."

Sinéad said she didn't want to be part of such a value system and so declined to take part in the awards ceremonies or to accept any awards she might be given.She must also have been aware that even if she did appear at the ceremonies anything she might say would be lost and edited from the televised ceremonies that would be broadcast. All except the Irish one, that is.

In a fax message to Sinéad O'Connor's home in Los Angeles that weekend, IRMA Award show TV producer David Blake Knox made an impassioned plea to Sinéad not to disappoint her Irish fans. It was pointed out to her that the show would be broadcast live, and that the awards were decided on merit since the shortlisted artists were chosen for awards by popular vote. A compromise was also suggested for the awards - Sinéad need not accept them but they could be handed to a popular radio host to be auctioned the following week for the Irish Society for the Prevention of Cruelty to Children. Further, she was told if she agreed to perform she was free to make any statement she saw fit. She agreed.

The following weekend Sinéad appeared in front of a live TV audience from the Point Depot in Dublin. Overcome by an overwhelming and emotional reception from the 5,000 strong crowd of screaming teenage fans, Sinéad broke down and wept. "No piece of metal or glass can make up for this," she sobbed. "A lot of people don't realise to be an artist is an enormous honour...," she said before pausing, her voice choked and shaking with emotion. "Whatever I give you, look how many there is of ye and there's only one of me and I'm getting it back off every one of you... don't be afraid to express yourselves no matter what the cost." Then she sang 'I Do Not Want What I Haven't Got'.

When the performance was finished the screaming uproar began again. Over the din Sinéad shouted, "Express your fucking selves no matter what the cost." Within seconds the TV company's switchboard was jammed with complaints from angry parents. Sinéad's essential message was lost in her own impetuosity.

That night she revealed to Donal White, an Irish radio news reporter, that she was seriously considering retiring from the business that had made her life a misery. "I like singing, I like expressing myself, but I don't like having to deal with some of the things that I have to deal with as a consequence of that. I'm not someone who is interested in commercial success. I happened to have a hit record but it won't happen again. It's not what I am into. I'm not doing what I'm doing in order to have hit records. I don't like being famous and I don't like the effect it's having on my life."

Significantly, Sinéad's husband John Reynolds was at the awards, the two having reconciled their differences and spent some time together in Los Angeles with their son, three year old Jake.

Two days later Sinéad kept her pledge not to appear at the British Music Awards, the Brits, whose organisers concocted their own spiteful tribute to her when she was awarded the Best International Female award. They played a video tape of Whitney Houston singing the American National Anthem, 'The Star Spangled Banner' at the 1991 Superbowl. It was a cheap shot, and Sinéad's record company voiced a strong objection after the event.

The organiser of the BBC Brits was the controversial deejay, *Sun* columnist and record producer Jonathan King who for reasons best

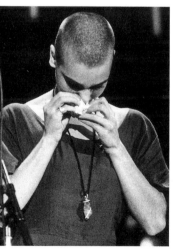

Sinéad at the 1991 IRMA Awards in Dublin.

Sinéad O'Connor \ Epilogue

Top: with fan after the IRMA Awards. Bottom: with younger brother John.

known to himself had been a champion of Sinéad O'Connor during 1990. The use of the Houston tape could have been his idea. If it was, it certainly gives truth to the axiom that "Hell hath no fury like an old queen scorned."

Sinéad's opinion of the BPI incident was summed up in a brief statement on her return to Los Angeles. "It vindicates everything I've been saying in the past two weeks about awards ceremonies," she said. "The most disgusting thing about the BPI show was the censorship," she added, referring to the ban on artists mentioning the Gulf War because it was 'too boring'.

In March Sinéad swept the *Rolling Stone* Readers' and Critics polls, thus ending all arguments that her career would be damaged by her controversial stance on so many different issues. She won Artist of the Year, Best Album, Best Female Singer and the critics' award for the Best Single.

The readers' vote meant more to her than the Grammys, she said, adding as an aside that she was proud to be regarded as a troublemaker. "It's a matter of actual people saying they like me. That's much more exciting, more real than the Grammys which are very political."

In an interview in the March 7 issue of *Rolling Stone*, which carried her picture on the cover for the second time in less than 12 months, there was also a hint of sadness amidst the jubiliation. Reflecting on the trauma filled year, she said she needed to return to normal. "I need to forget that I'm Sinéad O'Connor."

The interviewer asked her if she feels 'so different' now. She replied, "Oh yeah, I feel even more different now. Absolutely."

When people find time and understanding to deal with a shaven headed, outspoken 24 year old Irish woman of striking beauty with a truckload of opinions and attitudes in a manner more substantial and meaningful than the jerk of a knee, then perhaps some of her own wishes will have been fulfilled. But that's a tall order.

Discography

Singles

Troy/Still Listening
Ensign ENY 610 October 1987

Troy/Still Listening
Ensign ENYX 610 October 1987

Mandinka/Drink Before The War
Ensign ENY 611 December 1987
(Also available in gatefold sleeve)

Mandinka *(extended version)*/**Mandinka** *(dub mix)*/**Drink BeforeThe War**
Ensign ENYX 611 (12-inch) December 1987

Mandinka/Drink Before The War/Mandinka *(instrumental dub version)*/
Still Listening
Ensign ENYCD 611 (CD single) December 1987

Mandinka *(Jake's remix)*/**Mandinka/Drink Before The War**
Ensign ENYXR 611 (12-inch) December 1987

I Want Your (Hands On Me)/Just Call Me Joe
Ensign ENY 613 April 1988 *(With MC Lyte)*

I Want Your (Hands On Me) *(dance mix)*/**I Want Your (Hands On Me)** *(street mix)*/
I Want Your (Hands On Me) *(edited version)* /**Just Call Me Joe**
Ensign ENYX 613 (12-inch) April 1988 *(With MC Lyte)*

I Want Your (Hands On Me) *(dance mix)*/I **Want Your (Hands On
Me)** *(street mix)* /**I Want Your (Hands On Me)** *(edited version)* /**Just Call Me Joe**
Ensign ENYCD 613 (CD single) April 1988 *(With MC Lyte)*

I Want Your (Hands On Me) *(Knee-trembler mix)*/**I Want Your Hands On Me**
(Hickey On Me Neck mix)/**I Want Your (Hands On me)** *(edited version)*/
Just Call Me Joe
Ensign ENYXR 613 (12-inch) April 1988 *(With MC Lyte)*

Jump In The River/Never Get Old
Ensign ENY 618 October 1988

Jump In The River *(duet with Karen Finley)*/**Jump In The River/Never Get Old**
(live version)
Ensign ENYX 618 October 1988

Jump In The River *(duet with Karen Finley)*/**Jump In The River/Never Get Old**
(live version)
Ensign ENYCD 618 (CD single) October 1988

Nothing Compares 2U/Jump In The River
Ensign ENY 630 January 1990

Nothing Compares 2U/Jump In The River/Jump In The River *(instrumental)*
Ensign ENYX 630 *(12-inch)* January 1990

Nothing Compares 2U/Jump In The River/Jump In The River *(instrumental)*
Ensign ENYCD 630 (CD single) January 1990

Nothing Compares 2U/Jump In The River
Ensign ENYB 630 *(7-inch boxed set with poster and badge)*
January 1990

The Emperor's New Clothes/What Do You Want
Ensign ENY 633 July 1990

The Emperor's New Clothes/The Emperor's NewClothes *(Hank Shocklee remix)***/**
I Am Stretched On Your Grave*(Apple Brightness mix)***/I Am Stretched**
On Your Grave
(Night Until Morning dub mix)
Ensign ENYX 633 (12-inch) July 1990

The Emperor's New Clothes/The Emperor's New Clothes *(Hank Shocklee remix)***/**
I Am Stretched On Your Grave *(Apple Brightness mix)***/I Am Stretched**
On Your Grave
(NightUntil Morning dub mix)
Ensign ENYCD 633 (CD single) July 1990

The Emperor's New Clothes/What Do You Want/I Am Stretched
On Your Grave
Ensign ENYMC 633 *(cassette single)* July 1990

The Emperor's New Clothes/What Do You Want
Ensign ENYB 633 *(7-inch boxed set with poster and postcards)*
July 1990

Three Babies/Troy *(live version)*
Ensign ENY 635 October 1990

Three Babies/Damn Your Eyes/Troy *(live version)***/The Value Of Ignorance**
Ensign ENYX 635 October 1990

Three Babies/Damn Your Eyes/Troy *(live version)***/The Value Of Ignorance**
Ensign ENYCD (CD single) October 1990

Three Babies/Damn Your Eyes/Troy *(live version)*/ **The Value Of Ignorance**
Ensign ENYMC (cassette single) October 1990

Albums

THE LION AND THE COBRA
Jackie/Mandinka/Jerusalem/Just Like U Said It Would B/Never Get Old/Troy/
I Want Your (Hands On Me)/Drink Before TheWar/Just Call Me Joe
Ensign CHEN 7 January 1988

I DO NOT WANT WHAT I HAVEN'T GOT
Feel So Different/I Am Stretched On Your Grave/Three Babies/
The Emperor's New Clothes/Black Boys On Mopeds/Nothing Compares 2U/
Jump In The River/Last Day Of Our Acquaintance/I Do Not Want What I
Haven't Got
Ensign CHEN 14 March 1990